SUMMERTIME FUN COOKBOOK

**Great American Opportunities, Inc,/
Favorite Recipes® Press**

President: Thomas F. McDow III
Editorial Manager: Mary Jane Blount
Editors: Georgia Brazil,
Mary Cummings, Jane Hinshaw,
Linda Jones, Mary Wilson
Typography: Jessie Anglin,
Sara Anglin, Pam Newsome

This cookbook is a collection of our
favorite recipes which are not
necessarily original recipes.

Published by:
Favorite Recipes® Press, a division of
Great American Opportunities, Inc.
P. O. Box 305142
Nashville, Tennessee 37230

Manufactured in the United States of America
First Printing: 1993   40,000 copies

Contents

Summer Fun   4

Chill Out Fun   5

Photograph Recipes   6
Ice Creams   7
Frozen Desserts   11
Beverages   20
Fun! Fun! Fun!   30

Munchy Fun   31

Photograph Recipes   32
Cookies   33
Candies   43
Snacks   48
Fun! Fun! Fun!   58

Garden Patch Fun   59

Photograph Recipes   60
Jams and Jellies   61
Relishes   65
Fun! Fun! Fun!   68

Cook-Out Fun   69

Photograph Recipes   70
Main Dishes   71
Accompaniments   77
Fun! Fun! Fun!   80

Picnic Fun   81

Photograph Recipes   82
Appetizers   83
Sandwiches   84
Accompaniments   88
Fun! Fun! Fun!   93

Index   94

Summer Fun

To children, summers have a wonderful air of freedom and fun about them: time to do nothing but stretch out under a tree and read; time to laze about sharing a popsicle with friends; time to play out under street lights until called home for dinner; time to run through the sprinkler or bike to the corner for ice cream.

To adult "children," summer is when the living is a bit easier; softball games, flickering fireflies, and sweet-smelling gardens; lounging by the pool in search of a perfect tan; picnics, fireworks, tall frosty drinks.

For everybody, summer means wonderful foods to enjoy with family and friends at reunions, company picnics, camp cook-outs, Fourth of July block parties, ice cream socials and neighborhood barbecues. Entertaining is relaxing, spontaneous and fun. The secret is serving foods that can be prepared ahead, served cold or frozen, or cooked outdoors.

Inside our tall, cool pages, you'll find recipes for these and all of summer's lazy moments. For eating outdoors, *Picnic Fun* is loaded with ideas for packable take-along treats. And because we not only want to eat outdoors in summer but cook there as well, *Cook-Out Fun* features new recipes for outdoor favorites.

Look for easy cookies, candies and snacks in *Munchy Fun* and cool off with luscious frozen desserts and cold beverages in *Chill-Out Fun*. Then, try our easy ways to "put up" a variety of foods in *Garden Patch Fun* for great do-ahead gifts or just for a taste of summer during those winter months when you need it most.

CHILL OUT FUN

Frozen Desserts and Beverages

Neopolitan Ice Cream Sandwich Cake

1   10-ounce frozen loaf pound cake, partially thawed
2 cups vanilla ice cream, slightly softened
2 tablespoons HERSHEY'S strawberry syrup
2 tablespoons HERSHEY'S chocolate syrup

Remove cake from foil pan; line pan with plastic wrap. Slice cake horizontally into 3 layers. Place bottom cake layer back into prepared pan and place in freezer. Stir together 1 cup ice cream and strawberry syrup in small bowl. Spread over cake layer in pan. Place second cake layer on top of strawberry mixture; return to freezer. Stir together remaining 1 cup ice cream and chocolate syrup in small bowl. Spread over cake layer in pan. Top with third cake layer. Freeze, covered, until firm. Cut into slices. Serve frozen. **Yield:** 8 servings.

Frozen Fudge Sundae Dessert

2¼ cups finely crushed round butter crackers
½ cup butter or margarine, melted
1   18-ounce jar HERSHEY'S Chocolate Shoppe Topping
2 small packages vanilla instant pudding mix
1½ cups cold milk
1 quart vanilla ice cream, slightly softened
8 ounces whipped topping, thawed
12 to 15 maraschino cherries, drained (optional)

Stir together crushed crackers and butter. Press onto bottom of 9x13-inch dish. Spread fudge topping over crumbs. Stir together instant pudding mix, milk and ice cream in bowl until well blended; spread over mixture in dish. Top with whipped topping. Freeze, covered, until firm. Cut into pieces; garnish each piece with marashino cherry. Serve frozen. **Yield:** 12 to 15 servings.

Easy Homemade Chocolate Ice Cream

1 14-ounce can Eagle® Brand
   sweetened condensed milk
2/3 cup chocolate syrup
2 cups Borden® whipping cream,
   whipped

Combine condensed milk and syrup in bowl; mix well. Fold in whipped cream. Pour into 5x9-inch loaf pan or other 2-quart container; cover. Freeze for 6 hours or until firm. **Yield:** 1½ quarts.

French Vanilla: Omit syrup. Combine condensed milk, 3 beaten egg yolks and 4 teaspoons vanilla; mix well. Fold in whipped cream.

Peppermint Candy: Omit syrup. Combine condensed milk, 3 beaten egg yolks and 4 teaspoons vanilla; mix well. Fold in whipped cream and ¼ to ½ cup crushed hard peppermint candy.

Buttered Pecan: Omit syrup. Combine 2 tablespoons melted butter and ½ to ¾ cup chopped pecans. Combine with condensed milk, 3 beaten egg yolks and 1 teaspoon maple flavoring; mix well. Fold in whipped cream.

Mint Chocolate Chip: Omit syrup. Combine condensed milk, 3 beaten egg yolks, 2 teaspoons peppermint extract and 3 to 4 drops of green food coloring if desired; mix well. Fold in whipped cream and ½ cup miniature chocolate chips.

Coffee: Omit syrup. Combine condensed milk, 1 tablespoon instant coffee dissolved in 1 teaspoon hot water, 3 beaten egg yolks and 4 teaspoons vanilla; mix well. Fold in whipped cream.

Strawberry: Omit syrup. Blend one 10-ounce package thawed frozen strawberries in syrup until smooth. Combine with condensed milk, 3 beaten egg yolks, 1½ teaspoons vanilla and a few drops of red food coloring if desired; mix well. Fold in whipped cream.

Photograph for this recipe is on the cover.

CHILL OUT FUN

CHILL OUT FUN

The Best Ice Cream

4 eggs, beaten
1¼ cups sugar
1   14-ounce can sweetened condensed
    milk
2 cups half and half
1 teaspoon vanilla extract
¼ teaspoon salt
2 quarts (about) milk

Beat eggs with sugar, condensed milk, half and half, vanilla and salt in saucepan. Cook to 160 degrees, stirring constantly. Cool quickly in bowl of cold water, stirring constantly. Pour into ice cream freezer container. Add milk to fill line. Freeze using manufacturer's instructions. May add strawberries if desired. **Yield:** 8 servings.

Butter Pecan
Ice Cream

1 cup chopped pecans
5 eggs
2 cups sugar
1   14-ounce can sweetened condensed
    milk
2 teaspoons vanilla extract
2 teaspoons butter extract
2 teaspoons maple extract
2 cups whipping cream, whipped
4 to 5 cups milk

Spread pecans on baking sheet. Roast at 300 degrees for 10 minutes, stirring occasionally; set aside. Beat eggs with sugar in large bowl. Add condensed milk, vanilla, butter extract and maple extract; beat well. Fold in pecans and whipped cream. Pour into 1-gallon ice cream freezer container. Add milk to fill line. Freeze using manufacturer's instructions. **Yield:** 16 servings.

Ask several friends to bring a freezer full of their favorite homemade ice cream and have an old-fashioned ice cream social.

Cherry Mash
Ice Cream

4 eggs
1 1/2 cups sugar
2 cups whipping cream
1   14-ounce can sweetened condensed
   milk
2 tablespoons vanilla extract
1   12-ounce can evaporated milk
8 Cherry Mash candy bars
Whole milk

Beat eggs in large mixer bowl until foamy. Add sugar gradually, beating until thickened. Add whipping cream, condensed milk, vanilla and evaporated milk; mix well. Heat candy bars in saucepan until soft. Add to milk mixture; mix well. Pour into ice cream freezer container. Add whole milk to fill line. Freeze using manufacturer's instructions.
Yield: 4 to 6 servings.

Lemon Ice Cream

4 cups half and half
2 cups sugar
2 tablespoons freshly grated lemon rind
2/3 cup freshly squeezed lemon juice

Combine half and half and sugar in bowl, stirring until dissolved. Stir in lemon rind and juice. Pour into 9x13-inch pan or individual dessert dishes. Freeze for several hours or until firm.
Yield: 12 servings.

Strawberry Sorbet

1   20-ounce package frozen
   strawberries
1 1/4 cups apple juice
3 tablespoons strawberry jam
1/2 cup plain or strawberry yogurt

Combine strawberries, apple juice, jam and yogurt in blender container. Process until puréed. Pour into 2-quart container. Freeze, covered, until almost firm. Process in blender again for lighter texture. Pour into container. Freeze, covered, until firm. **Yield:** 8 servings.

CHILL OUT FUN

Strawberry Ice Cream

2 3-ounce packages vanilla instant
    pudding mix
4 cups milk
1 tablespoon vanilla extract
1 cup sweetened condensed milk
1 cup sugar
2 16-ounce packages frozen
    strawberries, thawed
Several drops of food coloring
5 to 6 cups milk

Combine pudding mix with 4 cups milk
in large bowl; mix well. Stir in vanilla,
condensed milk, sugar and strawberries.
Add enough food coloring to obtain
desired tint. Pour into 1-gallon ice cream
freezer container. Add remaining milk to
fill line. Freeze using manufacturer's instructions. **Yield:** 16 servings.

Old-Fashioned Vanilla Ice Cream

5 egg yolks
1½ cups sugar
1 cup whipping cream
1 12-ounce can evaporated milk
2 teaspoons vanilla extract
⅛ teaspoon salt
8 to 10 cups milk
5 egg whites

Beat egg yolks in bowl until frothy. Add
sugar, whipping cream and evaporated
milk. Beat well until sugar is dissolved.
Add vanilla, salt and half the milk; mix
well. Beat egg whites in mixer bowl until
stiff peaks form. Fold into milk mixture.
Pour into 1-gallon ice cream freezer container. Add milk to fill line. Freeze using
manufacturer's instructions.
Yield: 16 servings.

*Make a quick sauce for ice
cream by melting chocolate-
covered mint patties in the
microwave.*

Vanilla Ice Cream

8 eggs
4 cups sugar
1/8 teaspoon salt
1   12-ounce can evaporated milk
1   14-ounce can sweetened condensed
    milk
2 tablespoons vanilla extract
3 to 4 quarts milk

Beat eggs at high speed in mixer bowl until lemon-colored. Add sugar and salt. Beat until thickened. Stir in evaporated milk, condensed milk and vanilla. Pour into 2-gallon ice cream freezer container. Add milk filling 3/4 full. Freeze using manufacturer's instructions.
Yield: 24 servings.

Date-Pecan Ice Cream Topping

3/4 cup chopped dates
3/4 cup chopped pecans
3/4 cup flaked coconut
1 tablespoon thawed frozen orange
    juice concentrate

Combine dates, pecans, coconut and orange juice concentrate in bowl. Chill in refrigerator. **Yield:** 2 1/4 cups.

Buster Bar Dessert

32 ounces Oreo Cookies, crushed
1 gallon butter brickle ice cream,
    softened
1   16-ounce can chocolate syrup
2 bananas, sliced
12 ounces whipped topping
1 cup chopped pecans

Layer cookie crumbs and ice cream in 9x13-inch pan. Freeze until firm. Reserve 1/4 cup chocolate syrup. Drizzle remaining chocolate syrup over ice cream. Slice bananas over chocolate syrup. Freeze until firm. Top with whipped topping, pecans and reserved chocolate syrup. Freeze until serving time. May use vanilla ice cream if preferred. **Yield:** 15 servings.

CHILL OUT FUN

CHILL OUT FUN

Butter Brickle Dessert

1 cup cracker crumbs
1 cup graham cracker crumbs
½ cup melted margarine
2 cups milk
2 4-ounce packages vanilla instant
   pudding mix
½ gallon butter brickle ice cream,
   softened
8 ounces whipped topping
3 Heath candy bars, crushed

Combine cracker crumbs, graham cracker crumbs and melted margarine in bowl; mix well. Press into greased 9x13-inch baking dish. Bake at 350 degrees for 7 minutes. Cool to room temperature. Combine milk and pudding mix in mixer bowl. Beat at low speed for 2 minutes. Add softened ice cream. Spread on cooled crust. Chill in refrigerator until set. Spread whipped topping over dessert; sprinkle with crushed candy. Chill until serving time or freeze until firm. **Yield:** 15 servings.

Butterfinger Delight

2 cups graham cracker crumbs
6 tablespoons butter or margarine,
   softened
2 4-ounce packages vanilla instant
   pudding mix
2 cups milk
½ gallon vanilla ice cream, softened
2 large Butterfinger candy bars, crushed
8 ounces whipped topping
1 large Butterfinger candy bar, crushed

Mix cracker crumbs and butter in 9x13-inch dish; press evenly into dish. Combine pudding mix and milk in bowl; mix until smooth. Let stand for 5 minutes. Blend in ice cream. Fold in 2 crushed candy bars. Spoon into prepared dish. Freeze for 30 minutes. Top with whipped topping and remaining crushed candy bar. Store in refrigerator. **Yield:** 12 to 16 servings.

Butterscotch Dessert

1 cup melted margarine
2 cups flour
¹/₂ cup oats
¹/₂ cup packed light brown sugar
1 cup chopped pecans
1   16-ounce jar butterscotch sauce
1 pint vanilla ice cream, softened

Combine margarine, flour, oats, brown sugar and pecans in bowl; mix well. Pat into thin layer on baking sheet. Bake at 400 degrees for 15 minutes. Crumble while still hot. Sprinkle half the crumbs into 9x13-inch dish. Drizzle with half the butterscotch sauce. Spoon ice cream over sauce. Top with remaining crumbs and butterscotch sauce. Freeze until serving time. **Yield:** 15 servings.

Candy Bar Pie

1¹/₃ cups grated coconut
2 tablespoons melted butter
1 teaspoon instant coffee granules
2 tablespoons water
1   7¹/₂-ounce chocolate candy bar
4 cups whipped topping

Mix coconut and butter in bowl. Press into 8-inch pie plate. Bake at 325 degrees for 10 minutes or until coconut is golden brown. Cool to room temperature. Dissolve coffee granules in water in small saucepan. Add chocolate. Heat over low heat until chocolate melts, stirring to mix well. Cool to room temperature. Fold in whipped topping. Spoon into prepared pie plate. Freeze for several hours to overnight. Garnish with chocolate curls or toasted slivered almonds.
Yield: 8 servings.

Make an easy frozen dessert of torn angel food cake and softened coffee ice cream. Freeze in loaf pan lined with waxed paper and serve sliced with chocolate sauce.

CHILL OUT FUN

CHILL OUT FUN

Chocolate Ice Cream Dessert

½ 16-ounce package Oreo cookies, crushed
¼ cup melted margarine
½ gallon vanilla ice cream
1 12-ounce can evaporated milk
1 cup sugar
1 cup margarine
2 squares unsweetened chocolate

Combine cookie crumbs and ¼ cup melted margarine in bowl; mix well. Press into greased 9x13-inch dish. Chill in freezer. Cut ice cream into 1½-inch thick slices. Arrange over crumb crust. Freeze, covered, until firm. Combine evaporated milk, sugar, 1 cup margarine and unsweetened chocolate in saucepan. Cook over low heat for 15 to 20 minutes or until sugar is completely dissolved, stirring frequently. Chill in refrigerator until thickened. Spread over ice cream layer. Freeze, covered, until serving time. **Yield:** 15 servings.

Chocolate-Cherry Ice Cream Dessert

30 creme-filled chocolate sandwich cookies, crumbled
¼ cup melted margarine
½ gallon vanilla ice cream, softened
1 21-ounce can cherry pie filling

Reserve ¼ cup cookie crumbs. Combine remaining cookie crumbs with margarine in large bowl; mix well. Press over bottom of 9x13-inch dish. Chill for 10 to 15 minutes. Layer half the ice cream, pie filling, remaining ice cream and reserved crumbs in prepared dish. Freeze, covered, for 2 hours. Cut into squares. **Yield:** 12 to 15 servings.

For an easy refreshing dessert, shape scoops of lemon or orange sherbet into balls and roll in flaked coconut; freeze until firm. Serve over sliced strawberries or peaches.

Chocolate Malt Ice Cream Torte

1 cup finely crushed graham cracker
   crumbs
3 tablespoons sugar
1 teaspoon cinnamon
3 tablespoons melted butter or
   margarine, cooled
2 tablespoons finely grated semisweet
   chocolate
1/2 gallon vanilla or marble fudge ice
   cream
1/2 cup malted milk powder
4 ounces chocolate-covered malted
   milk balls, coarsely chopped

Combine crumbs, sugar and cinnamon
in bowl; mix well. Stir in butter and
chocolate until well mixed. Press onto
bottom and halfway up side of greased
springform pan. Let ice cream stand in
bowl until soft but not melted. Add
malted milk powder; beat until well
blended. Spread over crumb mixture.
Sprinkle with malted milk balls, patting
lightly into ice cream. Freeze, covered,
for 4 hours or until firm. Loosen from
side of pan with knife dipped in hot
water. Remove pan ring. Cut into
wedges. **Yield:** 10 to 12 servings.

Cool and Easy Ice Cream Dessert

2 cups semisweet chocolate chips
2 tablespoons margarine
4 1/2 cups crisp rice cereal
1/2 gallon mint chocolate chip ice
   cream, softened

Melt chocolate chips and margarine in
heavy saucepan, stirring occasionally.
Stir in cereal. Reserve 1/2 cup mixture.
Press remaining cereal mixture into 9x13-
inch dish. Spread with ice cream;
sprinkle with reserved cereal mixture.
Freeze for several hours. Let stand for
several minutes before serving.
Yield: 15 servings.

Crispy Ice Cream Dessert

3 cups crisp rice cereal
1 cup packed light brown sugar
1 cup coconut
½ cup chopped nuts
½ cup butter or margarine
½ gallon vanilla ice cream

Combine first 5 ingredients in bowl; mix well. Spread on baking sheet. Bake at 300 degrees for 20 minutes. Slice ice cream. Arrange slices in buttered dish. Top with cereal mixture. Freeze until serving time. **Yield:** 8 servings.

Mint Ice Cream Pies

¾ 16-ounce package Oreo cookies, finely crushed
½ cup melted butter or margarine
½ gallon mint ice cream
1   12-ounce jar caramel sauce
1   12-ounce jar hot fudge sauce
16 ounces whipped topping

Combine cookie crumbs and butter in bowl; mix well. Divide into 2 portions. Press each portion into 9-inch pie plate. Freeze until firm. Cut ice cream into slices; place on frozen crusts, smoothing tops. Combine sauces in bowl; mix well. Spread over pies. Freeze until firm. Top with whipped topping, swirling into peaks. Freeze until serving time. **Yield:** 16 servings.

Oreo-Cherry Delight

36 Oreo cookies, crushed
½ cup butter or margarine, softened
½ gallon vanilla ice cream
1 to 2   21-ounce cans cherry pie filling
4 cups whipped topping
Chocolate syrup
Chopped pecans

Combine cookie crumbs and butter in bowl; mix well. Press into 9x13-inch glass dish. Slice ice cream; arrange over crust. Layer pie filling and whipped topping over ice cream. Drizzle with chocolate syrup; sprinkle with pecans. Freeze, covered, until firm. Remove from freezer several minutes before serving. **Yield:** 8 to 10 servings.

Peanut Buster Parfait

1½ cups sweetened condensed milk
2 cups confectioners' sugar
⅔ cup chocolate chips
½ cup butter or margarine
1   16-ounce package Oreo cookies,
    crushed
½ cup butter or margarine, softened
2 cups Spanish peanuts
½ gallon vanilla ice cream, softened

Mix condensed milk and confectioners' sugar in saucepan Add chocolate chips and ½ cup butter. Simmer for 8 minutes, stirring constantly. Cool to room temperature. Combine cookie crumbs and remaining ½ cup butter in bowl; mix well. Press into 9x13-inch dish. Sprinkle with peanuts. Spread softened ice cream over cookie crust. Drizzle with chocolate mixture. Freeze until firm.
Yield: 12 servings.

Peppermint Ice Cream Pie

2 ounces unsweetened chocolate
¼ cup butter
⅔ cup sifted confectioners' sugar
2 tablespoons milk
1   3-ounce can coconut
1 quart peppermint ice cream, slightly
    softened

Melt chocolate and butter in double boiler over hot water. Remove from heat. Add mixture of confectioners' sugar and milk; mix well. Stir in coconut. Press in buttered pie plate. Chill until firm. Spoon ice cream into prepared pie plate. Freeze, covered with foil, until firm. Let stand for 30 minutes. **Yield:** 8 servings.

Dragon Dream Pops

1   16-ounce can water-pack peaches,
    drained
1   16-ounce can juice-pack crushed
    pineapple
2 ripe bananas

Purée peaches, undrained pineapple and bananas in blender. Pour into popsicle molds. Freeze until firm.
Yield: 20 servings.

CHILL OUT FUN

No-Drip Popsicles

1   3-ounce package fruit-flavored
    gelatin
1 package fruit-flavored drink mix
1 cup sugar
2 cups hot water
2 cups cold water
Drinking straws

Combine gelatin, drink mix, sugar and hot water in container with cover. Shake, covered, until well blended. Add cold water; mix well. Pour into ice cube tray. Freeze until partially set. Cut drinking straws into desired size for stick. Add 1 piece of straw to each cube section. Freeze until firm. May use gelatin and drink mix of same flavor or your choice of complimentary flavors. These popsicles will not drip while being eaten. **Yield:** 16 servings.

Brownie Ice Cream Sandwiches

1   21-ounce package fudge brownie mix
5 tablespoons flour
3/4 cup chocolate syrup
1/4 cup vegetable oil
1/4 cup water
1 egg
1 cup peanut butter chips
1 quart vanilla ice cream, softened

Combine first 6 ingredients in mixer bowl; beat well. Stir in peanut butter chips. Drop batter by tablespoonfuls onto greased cookie sheet. Bake at 350 degrees for 13 to 15 minutes. Cool on cookie sheet for several minutes. Remove to wire rack to cool completely. Spread ice cream 1/2 inch thick on half the cookies; top with remaining cookies. Wrap in waxed paper. Freeze until firm. **Yield:** 21 servings.

For easy popsicles, freeze fruit juice in popsicle molds or miniature paper cups. Children love them!

Chocolate-Coated Ice Cream Sandwiches

½ cup sugar
½ cup packed brown sugar
½ cup peanut butter
¼ cup shortening
¼ cup margarine, softened
1 egg
1¼ cups flour
¾ teaspoon baking soda
½ teaspoon baking powder
¼ teaspoon salt
1 pint ice cream or frozen yogurt
1 cup semisweet chocolate chips
2 tablespoons shortening

Combine first 5 ingredients in mixer bowl; mix well. Beat in egg. Add mixture of next 4 ingredients; beat well. Shape into 1¼-inch balls. Place 3 inches apart on nonstick cookie sheet. Flatten in crisscross pattern with floured fork. Bake at 375 degrees for 9 to 11 minutes or until brown. Cool in pan for several minutes. Remove to wire rack to cool completely. Press 1 slightly rounded tablespoon ice cream between 2 cookies. Repeat with remaining ice cream and cookies. Place on freezer tray. Freeze until firm. Melt chocolate chips and remaining 2 tablespoons shortening in saucepan over low heat, stirring occasionally. Remove from heat. Cool for 2 minutes. Dip each frozen sandwich into chocolate to coat both sides. Place on freezer tray. Freeze until firm. Store wrapped in plastic wrap. **Yield:** 15 servings.

Strawberry Delight

1 3-ounce package strawberry gelatin
1 cup boiling water
1 12-ounce angel food cake
1 10-ounce package frozen
   strawberries, thawed
½ gallon vanilla ice cream, softened

Dissolve gelatin in boiling water in bowl. Chill in refrigerator until partially set. Tear cake into bite-sized pieces. Add cake pieces and strawberries to gelatin; mix well. Fold in softened ice cream. Pour into tube pan. Freeze until firm. Immerse pan in hot water for 1 to 2 minutes; invert onto serving plate. Cut into slices to serve. **Yield:** 12 servings.

CHILL OUT FUN

Frozen Strawberry Squares

1 cup sifted flour
1/4 cup packed brown sugar
1/2 cup chopped walnuts
1/2 cup melted butter
2 egg whites
1 cup sugar
2 cups sliced strawberries
2 tablespoons lemon juice
1 cup whipping cream, whipped

Combine flour, brown sugar, walnuts and melted butter in bowl; mix well. Spread in shallow baking pan. Bake at 350 degrees for 20 minutes, stirring several times. Sprinkle 2/3 of the baked crumbs in buttered 9x13-inch baking dish. Beat egg whites in mixer bowl until soft peaks form. Add sugar, strawberries and lemon juice alternately, beating at high speed for 10 minutes. Fold whipped cream into mixture. Spread over crumbs. Sprinkle with remaining crumbs. Freeze, covered, for 6 hours. **Yield:** 15 servings.

Blueberry Mountain

1 cup fresh blueberries
4 cups milk
1/4 cup sugar
6 scoops vanilla ice cream

Rinse blueberries; drain. Combine blueberries, milk and sugar in blender container. Process until smooth. Pour into glasses. Top each with scoop of vanilla ice cream. **Yield:** 6 servings.

Kiwi-Yogurt Smoothie

2 kiwifruit, sliced
1 banana
1/4 cup plain low-fat yogurt
3 ice cubes
2 large strawberries

Combine kiwifruit, banana, yogurt and ice cubes in blender container. Process until puréed. Pour into 2 glasses. Garnish with strawberries. **Yield:** 2 servings.

Hawaiian Lemonade

1   6-ounce can frozen lemonade
    concentrate, thawed
1   12-ounce can unsweetened
    pineapple juice
1   12-ounce can apricot nectar
3/4 cup water
2   7-ounce bottles of ginger ale
Ice cubes

Mix lemonade concentrate, pineapple juice, apricot nectar and 3/4 cup water in large pitcher. Chill in refrigerator. Add ginger ale and ice cubes just before serving. **Yield:** 8 servings.

Sparkling Limeade

1 large lime
1/2 cup sugar
11/3 cups water
2 cups club soda
Pinch of salt

Place lime, sugar and water in blender container. Process at high speed for 30 seconds. Strain liquid into pitcher. Add club soda and salt. Serve immediately. **Yield:** 3 servings.

Mint Jewett

1 bunch mint leaves, finely chopped
1/2 cup lemon juice
1/2 cup water
11/2 cups sugar
11/2 to 2 quarts water

Combine mint leaves, lemon juice, 1/2 cup water and sugar in bowl. Let stand for 30 minutes. Add 11/2 to 2 quarts water; stir well. Serve over ice. **Yield:** 10 servings.

Orange Julius

1/4 cup sugar
1 cup milk
1 teaspoon vanilla extract
1   6-ounce can frozen orange juice
    concentrate
10 ice cubes

Combine first 4 ingredients in blender container. Process at high speed, adding ice cubes a few at a time until ice is crushed. **Yield:** 4 servings.

CHILL OUT FUN

Aloha Punch

2   6-ounce cans frozen orange juice
    concentrate, thawed
1½ cups water
1 cup crushed pineapple
⅓ cup lemon juice
½ cup sugar
2 liters ginger ale
Crushed ice

Combine orange juice concentrate, water,
pineapple, lemon juice and sugar in
punch bowl; mix until sugar dissolves.
Add ginger ale and ice just before serving. **Yield:** 12 servings.

Apple Punch

1   46-ounce can pineapple juice
1   12-ounce can frozen apple juice
    concentrate, thawed
1   12-ounce can frozen orange juice
    concentrate, thawed
3   1-liter bottles ginger ale, chilled

Combine pineapple juice, apple juice
concentrate and orange juice concentrate
in freezer container; mix well. Freeze for
2 days. Place mixture in punch bowl.
Add ginger ale 1 hour before serving.
Yield: 20 servings.

Coffee Punch

¾ cup instant coffee
2 cups sugar
2 cups water
6   12-ounce cans evaporated milk,
    chilled
½ gallon vanilla ice cream
2 quarts club soda, chilled

Combine instant coffee, sugar and water
in punch bowl; mix well. Add evaporated milk and ice cream, stirring gently
to mix. Pour in club soda.
Yield: 30 servings.

*For a refreshing spritzer, com-
bine equal parts ginger ale and
white grape juice. Serve over
crushed ice.*

Cranberry Punch

1 3-ounce package cherry gelatin
1 cup boiling water
3 cups cold water
1 6-ounce can frozen lemonade
concentrate
1 quart cranberry juice cocktail, chilled
Ice cubes
1 12-ounce bottle of ginger ale, chilled

Dissolve gelatin in boiling water in large punch bowl. Stir in cold water. Add lemonade concentrate, cranberry juice cocktail and ice. Add ginger ale just before serving. **Yield:** 25 servings.

Cranberry-Pineapple Punch

1 quart cranberry juice cocktail
1 quart pineapple juice
1½ cups sugar
1 tablespoon almond extract
2 quarts ginger ale, chilled

Combine cranberry juice, pineapple juice, sugar and almond extract in large pitcher; stir until sugar is dissolved. Store in airtight container in refrigerator until serving time. Pour cranberry mixture into punch bowl. Add ginger ale. Make ice ring with additional ginger ale to float in punch bowl. **Yield:** 25 servings.

Cranberry Sparkle Punch

1 6-ounce can frozen grape juice
concentrate, thawed
1 6-ounce can frozen lemonade
concentrate, thawed
1 6-ounce can frozen pink lemonade
concentrate, thawed
1 32-ounce bottle of cranberry juice
cocktail
1 6-ounce can frozen orange juice
concentrate, thawed
1 3-liter bottle of lemon-lime soda

Combine grape juice concentrate, lemonade concentrate, pink lemonade concentrate, cranberry juice cocktail and orange juice concentrate in large freezer container; mix well. Freeze until slushy. Spoon into punch bowl. Add lemon-lime soda; mix well. **Yield:** 40 servings.

Yellow Daffodil Punch

1   46-ounce can apricot nectar
1   46-ounce can pineapple-grapefruit
    juice
1   16-ounce can orange juice
    concentrate, thawed
1   1-quart bottle of 7-Up
1 quart pineapple sherbet

Combine first 3 ingredients in large
freezer container; mix well. Freeze until
firm. Thaw for 1 hour. Place in punch
bowl. Stir in 7-Up and sherbet just before
serving. **Yield:** 20 servings.

Easy Party Punch

2   3-ounce packages raspberry gelatin
1   3-ounce package cherry gelatin
3 cups boiling water
5 cups cold water
3 cups unsweetened pineapple juice,
    chilled
1   12-ounce can frozen orange juice
    concentrate, thawed
4 cups ice cubes
4 cups pineapple or lemon sherbet

Dissolve gelatins in boiling water in
large container. Add cold water, pineapple juice and orange juice concentrate;
mix well. Pour into punch bowl. Add ice
cubes; stir until ice cubes melt. Spoon
sherbet into punch. Serve immediately.
Yield: 32 servings.

Four-Fruit
Party Punch

3   46-ounce cans unsweetened
    pineapple juice
3   12-ounce cans frozen orange juice
    concentrate, thawed
3   12-ounce cans frozen lemonade
    concentrate, thawed
1   12-ounce can frozen limeade
    concentrate, thawed
15 cups water
4 quarts ginger ale, chilled
2 quarts club soda, chilled
1 quart orange sherbet

Mix first 5 ingredients in punch bowl.
Add ginger ale and club soda just before
serving. Float scoops of orange sherbet in
punch. **Yield:** 80 servings.

Garden Club Punch

3 pints frozen strawberries
2   46-ounce cans pineapple juice
2   46-ounce cans Hawaiian punch
1 quart ginger ale
1   12-ounce can frozen orange juice
    concentrate, prepared

Place frozen strawberries in punch bowl. Pour pineapple juice, Hawaiian punch, ginger ale and orange juice over strawberries. Let stand for 30 minutes or more before serving. Stir gently to mix. **Yield:** 60 servings.

Pineapple-Citrus Punch

1   16-ounce can pineapple juice
1   16-ounce can orange-grapefruit juice
Ice cubes
1   1-liter bottle of lemon-lime soda
1 cup lime sherbet

Mix juices in punch bowl. Add ice. Add lemon-lime soda and scoops of sherbet just before serving. **Yield:** 16 servings.

Perky Pink Punch

2   46-ounce cans pineapple-pink
    grapefruit juice, chilled
2 cups cranberry juice cocktail, chilled
1   28-ounce bottle of club soda, chilled
1 quart sherbet

Combine grapefruit juice, cranberry juice cocktail and club soda in punch bowl. Float scoopfuls of sherbet in punch. **Yield:** 25 servings.

Red Ice Cream Punch

1/2 gallon vanilla ice cream
2 packages strawberry-flavored drink
    mix
1 quart cold water
1 cup sugar
1   46-ounce can pineapple juice, chilled
2 quarts 7-Up or Sprite, chilled

Place ice cream in punch bowl. Mix drink mix, water and sugar in pitcher. Pour over ice cream. Add pineapple juice and 7-Up gradually, stirring slightly. **Yield:** 20 servings.

Slushy Fruit Punch

3 cups sugar
2 cups water
1/2 gallon raspberry sherbet
3 bananas
1   46-ounce can unsweetened
    pineapple juice
1   46-ounce can unsweetened orange
    juice
1   46-ounce can 7-flavor Hawaiian
    punch
1/2 cup lemon juice
3 quarts lemon-lime soda

Process sugar, water, sherbet, bananas, pineapple juice, orange juice, Hawaiian punch and lemon juice about 1/3 at a time in blender. Pour into 1 large or several small freezer containers. Freeze until firm. Let large container stand at room temperature for 1 hour or smaller containers for about 30 minutes or until slushy; do not thaw completely. Pour into punch bowl. Add lemon-lime soda to slush mixture just before serving. Garnish with fresh fruit of choice.
Yield: 50 servings.

Summer Fruit Punch

7 oranges, peeled and sectioned
1   16-ounce can frozen orange juice
    concentrate, thawed
6 cups unsweetened apple juice
1   46-ounce can unsweetened
    pineapple juice
7 medium bananas, mashed
Ginger ale or lemon-lime soda

Process oranges in food processor fitted with slicing blade. Add half the concentrate and juices. Process with plastic mixing blade for 2 to 3 seconds. Pour into large bowl. Add bananas, remaining concentrate and juices; mix well. Freeze in small plastic bowls until slushy. Remove from freezer 30 minutes before serving. Stir gently to evenly distribute fruits; add ginger ale. **Yield:** 25 to 35 servings.

Banana-Chocolate Shake

8 bananas, sliced
6 cups cold milk
1 cup chocolate instant drink mix
1 teaspoon vanilla extract
1½ pints vanilla ice cream

Combine bananas, cold milk, drink mix and vanilla ⅓ at a time in blender container. Process until smooth. Spoon into glasses. Top with scoops of ice cream. **Yield:** 8 servings.

Choco-Mint Shake

½ cup milk
¼ cup instant cocoa mix
1½ cups milk
½ teaspoon vanilla extract
⅛ teaspoon peppermint extract
2 cups vanilla ice cream

Microwave ½ cup milk for 1 minute or just until hot; pour into blender. Add cocoa mix; process until smooth. Add remaining 1½ cups milk and flavorings; blend well. Add ice cream; process until thick and smooth. **Yield:** 4 servings.

Cranberry-Cantaloupe Shake

3 cups chopped cantaloupe, chilled
¼ cup frozen cranberry juice
    concentrate
½ cup skim milk
½ cup vanilla low-fat yogurt

Combine cantaloupe, cranberry juice concentrate, milk and yogurt in blender container; process for 30 seconds. Serve in tall glasses. Garnish with sprinkle of nutmeg and cantaloupe chunks. **Yield:** 4 servings.

For a quick mocha shake, blend 1 pint coffee ice cream with 2 cups cold chocolate milk and ⅓ cup chocolate syrup. Serve in tall chilled glasses with dollop of whipped cream and sprinkle of cinnamon.

CHILL OUT FUN

Spiced Orange Frost

2 cups vanilla ice cream
1 6-ounce can frozen orange juice
    concentrate, thawed
1/8 teaspoon nutmeg
1/8 teaspoon cinnamon
2 cups cold milk
2 cups vanilla ice cream

Combine 2 cups ice cream, orange juice concentrate, nutmeg and cinnamon in mixer bowl; beat until smooth and well blended. Add milk gradually, beating constantly. Pour into chilled glasses. Top each with scoop of remaining 2 cups ice cream. Serve immediately.
Yield: 4 servings.

Strawberry Swirl

1 cup fresh strawberries
1 cup skim milk
1 cup strawberry yogurt
1 cup vanilla ice milk
1/4 cup sugar

Combine strawberries, milk, yogurt, ice milk and sugar in blender container. Process until smooth. Pour into glasses. Serve immediately. **Yield:** 6 servings.

Strawberry-Yogurt Shake

1/2 cup unsweetened pineapple juice
3/4 cup plain low-fat yogurt
11/2 cups thawed frozen unsweetened
    strawberries
1 teaspoon sugar

Combine pineapple juice, yogurt, strawberries and sugar in blender container. Process at medium speed until thick and smooth. Pour into tall glasses.
Yield: 2 servings.

Freeze lemonade and orange juice in ice trays to serve in iced tea.

Slush

2 12-ounce cans frozen orange juice
   concentrate
1 12-ounce can frozen lemonade
   concentrate
5 bananas
1 46-ounce can pineapple juice, chilled
6 cups cold water
1 1-liter bottle of lemon-lime or
   orange soda

Combine orange juice concentrate and lemonade concentrate in large container. Pour a small amount of mixture into blender container. Add bananas. Process until puréed. Add puréed bananas, pineapple juice and cold water to juice mixture; mix well. Freeze until slushy. Fill glass ¾ full with slush; add lemon-lime or orange soda. **Yield:** 18 servings.

Almond Tea

1 gallon hot tea
1 6-ounce can frozen orange juice
   concentrate
1 6-ounce can frozen lemonade
   concentrate
1½ cups sugar
2 teaspoons vanilla extract
1 tablespoon almond extract

Combine hot tea, orange juice concentrate, lemonade concentrate, sugar and flavorings in pitcher; mix well. Chill until serving time. May substitute 1½ cups lemon juice for frozen lemonade and 1 cup instant orange-flavored breakfast drink mix for orange juice.
Yield: 10 to 15 servings.

Tropical Tea

½ cup sugar
⅓ cup instant tea
1 cup instant orange drink mix
1 6-ounce can frozen pineapple juice
   concentrate
8 cups water

Combine sugar, instant tea and orange drink mix in pitcher; mix well. Add pineapple juice concentrate and water; mix well. Chill until serving time. Serve over ice. **Yield:** 8 servings.

CHILL OUT FUN

FUN! FUN! FUN!

"Keep your cool when the temperature soars!"

* Have a "Bring Your Own" ice cream party. Everyone brings a different topping or ice cream and makes a stupendous original sundae. Give a prize for the most original.

* Get goose bumps—Go see a scary movie.

* Make lemonade, the old-fashioned kind with real lemons—then drink it.

* Read *Snowbound* by John Greenleaf Whittier and shiver.

* Have a Christmas in July party. Rent a Christmas movie like *How the Grinch Stole Christmas*, *Home Alone* or *It's a Wonderful Life*.

* Freeze all the goodies you can think of—candy bars, fig cookies, grapes, strawberries, banana slices—and eat them frozen.

* Sit in front of the air conditioner or fan and look at ski vacation brochures or Christmas catalogs.

MUNCHY FUN

Cookies, Candies
and Snacks

S'More Cereal Squares

⅓ cup light corn syrup
3 1.65-ounce milk chocolate bars, broken
½ teaspoon vanilla extract
3½ cups honey graham cereal
1 cup miniature marshmallows

Bring corn syrup to a boil in 3-quart saucepan; remove from heat. Stir in chocolate bars and vanilla until chocolate is melted. Fold in cereal gradually until coated with chocolate. Fold in marshmallows. Press into buttered 4-inch square pan. Chill until firm. Cut into bars. Store in refrigerator.
Yield: 24 servings.

S'More Cookie Bars

½ cup butter or margarine
¾ cup sugar
1 egg
1 teaspoon vanilla extract
1⅓ cups unsifted all-purpose flour
¾ cup graham cracker crumbs
1 teaspoon baking powder
¼ teaspoon salt
4 1.65-ounce milk chocolate bars
1 cup marshmallow creme

Cream butter and sugar in mixer bowl until light and fluffy. Beat in egg and vanilla. Add mixture of flour, graham cracker crumbs, baking powder and salt; mix well. Spread half the dough in bottom of greased 8-inch square baking pan. Arrange candy bars over dough breaking as needed to fit. Spread with marshmallow creme. Scatter bits of remaining dough over marshmallow creme; spread carefully. Bake at 350 degrees for 30 to 35 minutes or until set. Cool in pan. Cut into squares. **Yield:** 16 servings.

Almond Bars

1   2-layer package yellow cake mix
1/3 cup margarine
1 cup ground almonds
1 cup confectioners' sugar
1 teaspoon almond extract
4 egg whites
1/2 cup chopped almonds

Mix cake mix and margarine in bowl until crumbly; reserve 1/2 cup. Press remaining crumbs into greased 9x13-inch baking pan. Combine 1 cup ground almonds, confectioners' sugar, flavoring and egg whites in mixer bowl. Beat at high speed for 4 minutes. Spoon into prepared pan. Sprinkle with mixture of reserved crumbs and 1/2 cup chopped almonds. Bake at 350 degrees for 20 to 30 minutes or until light golden brown. Cool in pan. Cut into bars.
Yield: 36 servings.

Applesauce Brownies

1 1/2 cups sugar
2 cups flour
1/2 cup shortening
2 eggs
1 3/4 cups applesauce
2 tablespoons baking cocoa
1/2 teaspoon cinnamon
1 1/2 teaspoons baking soda
1/2 teaspoon salt
2 tablespoons sugar
1/2 cup chocolate chips

Mix 1 1/2 cups sugar, flour, shortening, eggs, applesauce, baking cocoa, cinnamon, baking soda and salt in bowl. Spoon into greased 9x13-inch baking pan. Sprinkle with mixture of remaining 2 tablespoons sugar and chocolate chips. Bake at 350 degrees for 30 minutes or until edges pull from sides of pan.
Yield: 24 servings.

MUNCHY FUN

Brown Sugar Brownies

1/4 cup melted butter
1 cup packed brown sugar
1 egg
1 cup flour
1 teaspoon baking powder
1/2 teaspoon salt
1/2 cup chopped pecans

Combine melted butter and brown sugar in bowl; mix well. Cool. Beat in egg. Add flour, baking powder and salt; mix well. Stir in pecans. Spoon into greased 8x8-inch baking pan. Bake at 300 degrees for 30 to 45 minutes or until edges pull from sides of pan. **Yield:** 16 servings.

Cocoa Brownies

4 egg whites
1/2 cup canola oil
1 teaspoon vanilla extract
1 1/3 cups sugar
1/2 cup baking cocoa
1 1/4 cups flour
1/4 teaspoon salt

Beat egg whites in bowl until foamy. Beat in oil and vanilla. Stir in sugar, baking cocoa, flour and salt. Spoon into oiled 9x9-inch baking pan. Bake at 350 degrees for 22 to 26 minutes or until brownies spring back when lightly touched; do not overbake. **Yield:** 18 servings.

Pecan Brownies

1 3/4 cups sifted flour
1/4 teaspoon salt
1/2 teaspoon baking powder
1 cup chopped pecans
1 cup butter
4 ounces unsweetened chocolate
4 eggs
2 cups sugar
1 teaspoon vanilla extract

Sift first 3 ingredients together. Stir in pecans. Melt butter and chocolate in double boiler over hot water. Beat eggs in bowl. Add sugar gradually. Beat in chocolate mixture and vanilla. Stir in flour mixture. Spoon batter into oiled 9x13-inch baking pan. Bake at 350 degrees for 30 minutes. **Yield:** 48 servings.

Marshmallow Brownies

1 cup butterscotch chips
1/2 cup butter
1 1/2 cups flour
2/3 cup packed brown sugar
2 teaspoons baking powder
1/2 teaspoon salt
1 teaspoon vanilla extract
2 eggs
2 cups chocolate chips
1/2 cup chopped pecans
2 cups miniature marshmallows

Combine butterscotch chips and butter in 3-quart saucepan. Cook over medium heat until melted, stirring constantly. Cool. Add flour, brown sugar, baking powder and salt; mix well. Add vanilla, eggs, chocolate chips, pecans and marshmallows; mix just until moistened. Spoon into greased 9x13-inch baking pan. Bake at 350 degrees for 20 to 25 minutes; center will be partially set but will become firm when cool.
Yield: 15 servings.

Prize-Winning Butter Brickle Bars

1   2-layer package yellow cake mix
1/3 cup butter
1 egg, beaten
1   14-ounce can sweetened condensed milk
1 1/2 cups chopped pecans
1 cup brickle chips

Combine cake mix, butter and egg in bowl; mix well. Press into greased 11x15-inch baking pan. Combine condensed milk, pecans and brickle chips in bowl; mix well. Spoon evenly in prepared pan. Bake at 350 degrees for 20 to 25 minutes or until golden brown. Cool on wire rack. Cut into bars. **Yield:** 30 servings.

 Turn plain brownies into gourmet delights by slicing Snickers candy bars over freshly baked brownies. Return to oven until candy is softened and then spread over top. Cool and cut into squares.

MUNCHY FUN

Butterscotch Icebox Cookies

1/2 cup butter, softened
1 cup packed brown sugar
1 egg, beaten
1 teaspoon vanilla extract
1 1/2 cups flour
1/2 teaspoon baking soda
1/2 teaspoon cream of tartar
1/2 cup nuts

Cream butter and brown sugar in mixer bowl until light and fluffy. Add egg and vanilla; mix well. Sift flour, baking soda and cream of tartar into creamed mixture; mix well. Stir in nuts. Divide into 3 portions. Shape each into 1 1/4x12-inch roll. Wrap in waxed paper. Chill until firm. Cut into slices; place on greased cookie sheet. Bake at 350 degrees for 7 minutes or until brown.
Yield: 60 servings.

Chocolate Caramel Layer Squares

1/3 cup evaporated milk
1   14-ounce package caramels
1   2-layer package German chocolate
    cake mix
1/3 cup evaporated milk
3/4 cup butter
1 cup chopped nuts
1 cup semisweet chocolate chips

Combine 1/3 cup evaporated milk and caramels in microwave-safe bowl. Microwave for 3 minutes or until caramels are melted, stirring several times. Combine cake mix, 1/3 cup evaporated milk and butter in bowl; mix well with pastry blender. Spread half the chocolate mixture into greased 9x13-inch baking dish. Bake at 350 degrees for 6 minutes. Layer nuts, chocolate chips and caramel mixture over baked layer. Spoon remaining chocolate mixture over top. Bake at 350 degrees for 15 to 20 minutes.
Yield: 12 servings.

Chocolate Chip Cookies

1 2-layer package yellow or white
   cake mix
2 eggs
1/2 cup oil
1 cup chocolate chips

Combine cake mix, eggs and oil in large bowl; stir until moistened. Stir in chocolate chips. Drop by 2 tablespoonfuls 2 inches apart onto nonstick cookie sheet. Bake at 350 degrees for 15 minutes. Remove to wire rack to cool.
Yield: 36 servings.

Chocolate Chip Squares

2 20-ounce packages chocolate chip
   refrigerator cookie dough
16 ounces cream cheese, softened
2 cups sugar
3 eggs

Freeze cookie dough until firm. Cut 1 package dough into slices. Press into greased 9x13-inch baking dish. Combine cream cheese and sugar in mixer bowl; beat well. Beat in eggs 1 at a time. Pour into prepared dish. Cut remaining dough into slices; arrange on top. Bake at 350 degrees for 45 minutes. Cool. Cut into squares. **Yield:** 15 servings.

Chocolate Dump Bars

2 cups sugar
1³/₄ cups flour
5 eggs
1 cup oil
1/2 cup baking cocoa
1 teaspoon vanilla extract
1 teaspoon salt
1 cup chocolate chips
1 cup chopped walnuts

Mix sugar, flour, eggs, oil, baking cocoa, vanilla and salt in bowl until moistened. Spread into greased 9x13-inch baking pan. Sprinkle with chocolate chips and walnuts. Bake at 350 degrees for 30 minutes or until edges pull from sides of pan. Cool on wire rack. Cut into bars. **Yield:** 24 servings.

MUNCHY FUN

Chocolate-Peanut Butter Bars

1 cup peanut butter
6 tablespoons margarine, softened
1¼ cups sugar
3 eggs
1 teaspoon vanilla extract
1 cup flour
¼ teaspoon salt
2 cups chocolate chips

Cream peanut butter and margarine in mixer bowl until light and fluffy. Add sugar, eggs and vanilla; beat until creamy. Stir in flour, salt and 1 cup chocolate chips. Spread in ungreased 9x12-inch baking pan. Bake at 350 degrees for 25 to 30 minutes or until edges begin to brown. Top with remaining 1 cup chocolate chips. Let stand for 5 minutes. Spread melted chocolate over top. Cool completely. Cut into bars. **Yield:** 18 servings.

Lace Cookies

½ cup sugar
½ cup flour
½ cup quick-cooking oats
½ cup melted butter
½ teaspoon baking powder
1 teaspoon salt
2 tablespoons cream
2 tablespoons molasses
1 teaspoon vanilla extract

Combine sugar, flour, oats and melted butter in bowl; mix well. Add baking powder, salt, cream, molasses and vanilla; mix well. Drop by teaspoonfuls 2 inches apart onto ungreased cookie sheet. Bake at 325 degrees for 10 minutes or until edges are brown. Cool on cookie sheet for several minutes; remove with spatula to wire rack to cool completely. **Yield:** 32 servings.

Gooey Butter Cake Bars

1 2-layer package butter-recipe yellow
  cake mix
1/2 cup margarine, softened
1 egg
8 ounces cream cheese, softened
2 eggs
1 1-pound package confectioners'
  sugar

Combine cake mix, margarine and 1 egg
in bowl; mix until crumbly. Reserve 1/2
cup crumb mixture. Press remaining
crumb mixture into greased 9x13-inch
baking dish. Combine cream cheese and
2 eggs in mixer bowl; beat well. Add
confectioners' sugar gradually, beating
well after each addition. Pour into
prepared pan; sprinkle reserved crumb
mixture over top. Bake at 300 degrees for
1 hour. Cool completely. Cut into bars.
Bars will rise during baking and fall
while cooling. **Yield:** 24 servings.

Easiest Lemon Cookies

1 2-layer package pudding-recipe
  lemon cake mix
4 ounces whipped topping
1 egg
1 cup confectioners' sugar

Combine cake mix, whipped topping
and egg in bowl; mix well. Shape into
balls. Roll in confectioners' sugar. Place
on greased cookie sheet. Bake at 350
degrees for 13 to 15 minutes or until light
brown. Remove to wire rack to cool.
Yield: 36 servings.

*Make Lemon or Chocolate Gooey
Butter Cake Bars by substituting
lemon or chocolate butter-recipe
cake mix for yellow cake mix.*

MUNCHY FUN

MUNCHY FUN

Lemon Squares

1 cup flour
¼ cup confectioners' sugar
½ cup butter
2 eggs
1 cup sugar
½ teaspoon baking powder
2½ tablespoons fresh lemon juice
Salt to taste
Confectioners' sugar

Combine flour and ¼ cup confectioners' sugar in bowl; mix well. Cut in butter until crumbly. Press into greased 8x8-inch baking pan. Bake at 350 degrees for 20 minutes. Combine eggs, sugar, baking powder, lemon juice and salt in mixer bowl; beat well. Pour over baked layer. Bake at 350 degrees for 20 to 25 minutes or until set. Cool in pan. Cut into squares. Sprinkle with sifted confectioners' sugar. **Yield:** 16 servings.

Oh Henry Bars

4 cups oats
1 cup melted margarine
½ cup light corn syrup
1 cup packed brown sugar
1 cup chocolate chips
¾ cup peanut butter

Combine oats, margarine, corn syrup and brown sugar in large bowl; mix well. Spread in greased 11x17-inch baking pan. Bake at 350 degrees for 8 minutes or until light brown. Cool on wire rack. Melt chocolate chips with peanut butter in saucepan; blend well. Spread over baked layer. Cool. Cut into bars. **Yield:** 40 servings.

Easy Peanut Butter Cookies

1 cup sugar
1 cup peanut butter
1 egg
1 teaspoon vanilla extract

Mix sugar, peanut butter, egg and vanilla in bowl with spoon. Shape into 1-inch balls; place on nonstick cookie sheet. Bake at 300 degrees for 15 to 18 minutes or until light brown. Remove to wire rack to cool. **Yield:** 24 servings.

Potato Chip Cookies

1 cup butter, softened
1/2 cup sugar
1 teaspoon vanilla extract
1/2 cup crushed potato chips
1/2 cup chopped walnuts
2 cups flour

Cream butter, sugar and vanilla in mixer bowl until light and fluffy. Add potato chips, walnuts and flour; mix well. Shape mixture into 1-inch balls. Arrange on cookie sheet. Press flat with glass dipped in sugar. Bake at 350 degrees for 13 to 14 minutes or until golden brown.
Yield: 24 servings.

Presto Snack Bars

2 cups oats
1/3 cup packed brown sugar
1/3 cup butter, softened
1/4 cup honey
1/3 cup chocolate chips
1/4 cup peanut butter
1/4 cup chopped peanuts

Mix oats, brown sugar, butter and honey in large glass bowl. Microwave on High for 3 1/2 to 4 1/2 minutes or until bubbly, stirring every minute. Press firmly over bottom of 7x11-inch dish. Combine chocolate chips and peanut butter in small glass bowl. Microwave on High for 1 minute, stirring after 30 seconds. Spread over oats mixture; sprinkle with peanuts. Chill until firm. Cut into bars. Store in airtight container in refrigerator.
Yield: 30 servings.

Sour Cream Cookies

2 cups sugar
1 cup sour cream
3 1/2 cups flour
1 cup margarine, softened
1 teaspoon baking soda

Combine all ingredients in bowl; mix well. Drop by teaspoonfuls onto greased cookie sheet; press with fork. Bake at 400 degrees for 8 minutes. Cool on wire rack.
Yield: 5 dozen.

MUNCHY FUN

MUNCHY FUN

Soda Cracker Caramel Bars

34 soda crackers
1 cup butter
1 cup packed brown sugar
2 cups milk chocolate chips
1/2 cup chopped pecans

Layer crackers in bottom of foil-lined 9x13-inch baking dish. Melt butter in saucepan over medium heat. Stir in brown sugar. Bring to a boil, stirring frequently. Simmer for 3 to 5 minutes. Pour mixture over crackers. Bake at 400 degrees for 5 to 7 minutes. Sprinkle with chocolate chips. Let stand for 5 minutes. Spread melted chocolate over top. Sprinkle with pecans. Chill in refrigerator until set. Break or cut into bars.
Yield: 15 servings.

Perfect Sugar Cookies

1 cup butter, softened
1 cup oil
1 cup sugar
1 cup confectioners' sugar
2 teaspoons vanilla extract
1 teaspoon baking soda
1 teaspoon cream of tartar
2 eggs
1/4 teaspoon salt
4 cups flour

Cream butter, oil, sugar and confectioner' sugar in large mixer bowl until light. Add vanilla, baking soda, cream of tartar, eggs and salt; mix well. Add flour 1 cup at a time, mixing well after each addition. Chill for 4 hours or longer. Shape into small balls. Place on cookie sheet; flatten with bottom of glass dipped in sugar. Bake at 350 degrees for 10 to 13 minutes or until light brown. Remove to wire rack to cool. May add 1 tablespoon cinnamon if desired.
Yield: 100 servings.

Swedish Jam Bars

1   2-layer package yellow cake mix
1/2 cup chopped pecans
1/4 cup margarine, softened
1 egg, beaten
1   10-ounce jar apricot preserves

Combine cake mix, pecans, margarine
and egg in large mixer bowl. Beat at low
speed until mixture is crumbly. Press
into greased and floured 9x13-inch
baking pan. Spread preserves over top.
Bake at 350 degrees for 20 to 25 minutes
or until light brown. Cool on wire rack.
May top with favorite frosting or glaze
if desired. Cool completely before cutting into bars. **Yield:** 36 servings.

Captain Crunch Candy

2 cups white chocolate chips
1 1/2 cups Captain Crunch cereal
1 1/2 cups Rice Krispies cereal
1 cup unsalted dry roasted peanuts

Melt white chocolate chips in top of
double boiler over boiling water, stirring
occasionally. Combine cereals and
peanuts in large bowl; toss to mix. Pour
melted white chocolate over mixture,
stirring to coat cereal and peanuts. Drop
by teaspoonfuls onto waxed paper,
pressing lightly into shape with fingers.
Cool until set. **Yield:** 42 servings.

Chocolate-Oatmeal Candy

1/2 cup butter
1/2 cup milk
2 cups sugar
1 cup coconut
1/4 cup baking cocoa
3 cups oats
1 teaspoon vanilla extract

Bring butter, milk and sugar to a boil in
saucepan. Cook for 1 minute; remove
from heat. Stir in coconut, baking cocoa,
oats and vanilla. Drop by spoonfuls onto
waxed paper. Let stand until firm.
Yield: 24 servings.

MUNCHY FUN

MUNCHY FUN

Double-Decker Fudge

1 cup peanut butter chips
1   14-ounce can sweetened condensed
    milk
1/2 teaspoon vanilla extract
1 cup chocolate chips
1/2 teaspoon vanilla extract

Combine peanut butter chips and 2/3 cup condensed milk in small glass bowl. Microwave on High for 1 to 1 1/2 minutes or until melted, stirring after 1 minute. Stir in 1/2 teaspoon vanilla. Spread evenly in 8x18-inch dish. Combine remaining condensed milk and chocolate chips in glass bowl. Microwave on High for 1 to 1 1/2 minutes or until melted, stirring after 1 minute. Stir in 1/2 teaspoon vanilla. Spread over peanut butter layer. Chill, covered, until firm. Cut into 1-inch squares. Store in refrigerator.
Yield: 64 servings.

Foolproof Chocolate Fudge

3 cups semisweet chocolate chips
1   14-ounce can sweetened condensed
    milk
1/8 teaspoon salt
1/2 to 1 cup chopped pecans
1 1/2 teaspoons vanilla extract

Combine chocolate chips, condensed milk and salt in heavy saucepan. Cook over low heat until chocolate is melted, stirring frequently. Stir in pecans and vanilla. Pour into waxed paper-lined 9x9-inch pan. Chill in refrigerator for 2 hours. Invert onto cutting board; peel off waxed paper. Cut into squares. Store, loosely covered, at room temperature.
Yield: 60 servings.

Microwave Fudge

1 12-ounce jar chunky peanut butter
2 cups semisweet chocolate chips
1 14-ounce can sweetened condensed
   milk

Remove lid from peanut butter jar. Microwave peanut butter, loosely covered with plastic wrap, on High for 1 to 2 minutes or until peanut butter is easily removed from jar. Combine peanut butter, chocolate chips and condensed milk in 2-quart glass bowl. Microwave, covered, on High for 1 to 2 minutes or until chocolate chips are melted. Do not boil. Mix well. Pour into buttered 7x11-inch dish. Cool. Cut into squares. **Yield:** 15 servings.

Graham Toffee Squares

30 graham cracker squares
¾ cup butter
1 cup packed brown sugar
1 cup chopped pecans

Line greased 10x15-inch baking pan with graham crackers. Combine butter and brown sugar in saucepan. Boil for 2 minutes. Stir in pecans. Pour over crackers. Bake at 350 degrees for 10 minutes. Cut into small squares while warm. Remove to wire rack to cool.
Yield: 60 servings.

Hopscotch Crunchies

1 cup butterscotch chips
½ cup peanut butter
1 cup miniature marshmallows, melted
1 3-ounce can chow mein noodles

Combine butterscotch chips and peanut butter in glass dish. Microwave on Medium-High until melted; mix well. Stir in marshmallows and noodles. Drop by teaspoonfuls onto waxed paper. Let stand until firm. **Yield:** 36 servings.

Coconut-Peanut Butter Balls

2 cups shredded coconut
1/2 cup chunky peanut butter
4 teaspoons vanilla extract

Combine coconut, peanut butter and vanilla in bowl; mix well. Shape into small balls. Arrange on waxed paper-lined tray. Chill, covered, until firm. **Yield:** 2 dozen.

Peanut Butter Balls

1/2 cup peanut butter
1/4 cup dry milk powder
1/4 cup raisins
1 tablespoon honey

Combine peanut butter, dry milk powder, raisins and honey in bowl; mix well. Shape into balls. Chill until serving time. May coat with 1/4 cup chopped nuts, coconut or cereal if desired. **Yield:** 6 servings.

Peanut Butter Bonbons

2 tablespoons butter, softened
1 cup confectioners' sugar
1 cup chunky peanut butter
1 1/2 cups crisp rice cereal
8 ounces milk chocolate, melted

Combine butter, confectioners' sugar and peanut butter in bowl; mix well. Mix in cereal. Chill for 30 minutes or longer. Shape into small balls. Chill for 30 minutes longer. Dip into chocolate, coating well. **Yield:** 24 servings.

Peanut Butter Candy

1 cup melted margarine
1 teaspoon vanilla extract
1 cup peanut butter
1 1-pound package confectioners' sugar

Combine margarine, vanilla and peanut butter in bowl; mix well. Add confectioners' sugar gradually, beating well after each addition. Press into greased 9x13-inch glass dish. Chill in refrigerator. Cut into squares. **Yield:** 60 servings.

Peanut Butter Chews

1 cup light corn syrup
1 cup sugar
1 cup peanut butter
4 cups cornflakes
1 cup Spanish peanuts

Combine corn syrup and sugar in saucepan. Bring to a boil, stirring constantly. Remove from heat. Stir in peanut butter until melted. Add mixture of cornflakes and peanuts; mix well. Spoon into mounds on waxed paper. Let stand until set. **Yield:** 25 servings.

Mashed Potato Candy

1/2 cup cold mashed potatoes
1/4 teaspoon vanilla extract
1   1-pound package confectioners' sugar
1 cup peanut butter

Combine mashed potatoes and vanilla in bowl; mix well. Beat in confectioners' sugar a small amount at a time until mixture is the consistency of bread dough. Roll out on confectioners' sugar-coated surface. Spread with peanut butter. Roll as for jelly roll to enclose peanut butter. Cut into slices; place on waxed paper. Chill in refrigerator until set.
Yield: 24 servings.

Microwave Pralines

1   1-pound package light brown sugar
1 cup whipping cream
1 teaspoon vanilla extract
2 tablespoons margarine, softened
2 cups pecan halves

Mix brown sugar and whipping cream in glass bowl. Microwave on High for 8 to 12 minutes or until mixture boils. Add vanilla and margarine, stirring well. Add pecan halves. Drop by spoonfuls onto waxed paper. Chill until firm.
Yield: 3 dozen.

Rocky Road Candy

2 cups semisweet chocolate chips
1   14-ounce can sweetened condensed
    milk
2 tablespoons butter or margarine
1   10-ounce package miniature
    marshmallows
1   8-ounce jar unsalted roasted peanuts

Cook chocolate chips, condensed milk and butter in saucepan over low heat until chocolate chips are melted, stirring constantly; remove from heat. Combine marshmallows and peanuts in bowl. Fold in chocolate mixture. Line 9x13-inch pan with waxed paper, extending edges over sides. Spread mixture in pan. Chill until firm. Remove from pan; peel off waxed paper. Cut into 1-inch squares; wrap in plastic wrap. **Yield:** 8 dozen.

Chunky Puppy Chow

2 cups chocolate chips
1/2 cup margarine
1 cup chunky peanut butter
1   12-ounce package Crispix cereal
2 to 3 cups confectioners' sugar

Combine chocolate chips, margarine and peanut butter in large microwave-safe bowl. Microwave on High for 3 minutes or until melted. Add cereal, stirring to coat. Pour into large paper bag. Add confectioners' sugar; shake to coat. Store in airtight container. **Yield:** 16 servings.

Poppy Chow

4 cups Sugar Pops cereal
4 cups crisp rice cereal
1 package round pretzels
2 cups unsalted peanuts
1 1/2 pounds almond bark, melted

Combine cereals, pretzels and peanuts in bowl; toss lightly. Pour almond bark over mixture; toss gently to mix. Spoon onto greased waxed paper. Cool. Store in airtight container. **Yield:** 8 servings.

Sweet Crispix Mix

2   12-ounce packages Crispix cereal
2 cups pecan halves
2 cups almonds
14 tablespoons butter
2 cups packed light brown sugar
1 cup dark corn syrup
1½ to 2 teaspoons vanilla extract

Combine cereal, pecan halves and almonds in roasting pan sprayed with
nonstick cooking spray. Melt butter in
medium saucepan. Add brown sugar,
stirring until dissolved. Stir in corn
syrup. Bring to a boil over low heat, stirring constantly; remove from heat. Stir
in vanilla. Pour over cereal mixture; toss
to coat. Bake at 250 degrees for 1 hour,
stirring every 15 minutes. Spread on
10x15-inch baking sheets. Cool. Break
into large pieces. Store in airtight container. **Yield:** 12 servings.

My Favorite Trash

½ cup butter
13 ounces nutella hazelnut spread
2 teaspoons almond extract
1   14-ounce package honey-graham
    Chex cereal
1 pound dark raisins
8 ounces chopped dates
4 cups mixed nuts
2 cups semisweet chocolate chips
1   1-pound package confectioners'
    sugar

Melt butter in small saucepan. Add
nutella and almond extract; mix well.
Combine cereal, raisins, dates, mixed
nuts and chocolate chips in heavy duty
plastic garbage bag. Pour nutella mixture
over top; shake to coat. Add confectioners' sugar; shake to coat. Store in
airtight containers. May substitute
peanut butter for nutella.
Yield: 12 servings.

MUNCHY FUN

MUNCHY FUN

White Chocolate Crunch

1 14-ounce package Honeycomb cereal
1 12-ounce package pretzels
12 ounces mixed nuts
1½ to 2 pounds white chocolate candy
    coating
Candy sprinkles

Mix cereal, pretzels and nuts in very large bowl. Melt white chocolate in double boiler over hot water. Pour over cereal; stir to coat well. Spread on waxed paper. Sprinkle with candy sprinkles. Cool completely. Store in airtight container. **Yield:** 32 cups.

Yummy Bars

1 8-ounce chocolate candy bar
1 cup peanut butter
1 cup miniature marshmallows
3 cups crisp rice cereal

Combine candy bar, peanut butter and marshmallows in saucepan. Heat until melted, stirring to mix well. Fold in cereal. Press into greased 9x9-inch dish. Let stand until cool. Cut into bars. **Yield:** 30 servings.

Sweet and Spicy Almonds

3 tablespoons vegetable oil
2 cups whole blanched almonds
½ cup sugar
1½ teaspoons salt
1½ teaspoons cumin
¼ to 1 teaspoon cayenne pepper
1 tablespoon sugar

Heat oil in skillet. Stir in almonds and ½ cup sugar. Cook for 10 minutes or until almonds are golden brown, stirring frequently. Pour into bowl. Sprinkle with mixture of salt, cumin, cayenne pepper and 1 tablespoon sugar; toss to coat. Spread in single layer on waxed paper-lined surface. Let stand until cool. Store in airtight container. **Yield:** 2 cups.

Can't-Just-Eat-One Crackers

3/4 cup oil
1 envelope ranch salad dressing mix
1/4 teaspoon garlic powder
1/2 teaspoon lemon pepper
1 16-ounce package oyster crackers

Combine oil, salad dressing mix, garlic powder and lemon pepper in bowl; whisk until smooth. Add crackers, mixing to coat evenly. Spread on baking sheet. Bake at 275 degrees for 15 to 20 minutes or until golden brown.
Yield: 16 servings.

Mini Ritz Cracker Snack

3/4 cup vegetable oil
1 small envelope ranch-style
   buttermilk dressing mix
1/4 teaspoon garlic powder
1/2 teaspoon dillweed
1/4 teaspoon lemon pepper
2 12-ounce packages mini Ritz crackers

Combine oil, salad dressing mix, garlic powder, dillweed and lemon pepper in baking pan; mix well. Add mini Ritz crackers; mix well. Bake at 350 degrees for 20 minutes, stirring occasionally. Cool completely. Store in airtight container. **Yield:** 6 cups.

Easy Cheese Straws

1 6-ounce jar Old English sharp
   cheese spread, softened
1 11-ounce package pie crust mix

Combine cheese spread and pie crust mix in bowl; mix until smooth. Place in cookie press. Press into desired shapes on baking sheet. May roll into straws by hand. Bake at 300 degrees for 10 to 12 minutes or just until light brown. Remove to wire rack to cool. Store in airtight container. **Yield:** 3 dozen.

MUNCHY FUN

Dilly Smackers

1 package oyster crackers
2/3 cup corn oil
2 tablespoons dillweed
1 envelope ranch salad dressing mix

Place crackers in bowl. Combine oil, dillweed and salad dressing mix in small bowl; mix well. Pour over crackers; toss lightly. Spoon into ziplock storage bag. Let stand overnight before serving. **Yield:** 12 servings.

Granola

2¹/₂ cups oats
1 cup coconut
¹/₂ cup chopped pecans
¹/₂ cup wheat germ
¹/₄ cup vegetable oil
¹/₂ cup honey
¹/₂ teaspoon vanilla extract
1 cup raisins

Combine oats, coconut, pecans and wheat germ in large bowl; mix well. Add mixture of oil, honey and vanilla; mix well. Pour into large shallow baking pan. Bake at 250 degrees for 40 minutes, stirring every 15 minutes. Stir in raisins. Cool to room temperature, stirring occasionally. Store in airtight container. **Yield:** 20 servings.

Mexican Munch

1 3-ounce can French-fried onions
2 cups rice Chex cereal
1 4-ounce can potato sticks
³/₄ cup Spanish peanuts
¹/₄ cup melted butter
¹/₂ envelope taco seasoning mix

Combine onions, cereal, potato sticks and peanuts in 9x13-inch baking pan. Drizzle with butter; toss gently to mix. Sprinkle with taco seasoning mix; mix well. Bake at 300 degrees for 30 minutes, stirring occasionally. Cool. Store in airtight container. **Yield:** 14 servings.

Spiced Mixed Nuts

1/2 cup vegetable oil
12 cups mixed nuts
1 tablespoon celery seed
1 tablespoon garlic salt
3 tablespoons Worcestershire sauce
1 tablespoon Tabasco sauce

Mix oil and mixed nuts in 9x13-inch baking pan. Sprinkle with mixture of celery seed and garlic salt. Drizzle with mixture of Worcestershire sauce and Tabasco sauce; toss to mix well. Bake at 225 degrees for 1 1/2 hours, stirring every 15 minutes. Cool completely. Store in airtight container. **Yield:** 12 cups.

Nibble Mix

1 cup margarine
1/2 teaspoon garlic salt
1/4 teaspoon minced garlic
1 teaspoon salt
1 teaspoon curry powder
1 teaspoon Worcestershire sauce
Tabasco sauce to taste
5 cups mixed nuts
1 quart popped popcorn
1   12-ounce package corn chips
8 ounces small cheese crackers

Melt margarine in roasting pan in oven. Stir in next 6 ingredients. Add mixed nuts, popcorn, corn chips and crackers; toss gently. Bake at 250 degrees for 1 hour, stirring occasionally. Remove to paper towels to cool. **Yield:** 25 servings.

Niblets

6 ounces pretzel sticks
1 pound salted peanuts
1   12-ounce package rice Chex cereal
1   12-ounce package Cheerios
1 tablespoon (scant) each garlic salt,
   onion salt and celery salt
3 tablespoons Worcestershire sauce
1 cup melted butter

Combine pretzel sticks, peanuts and cereals in roasting pan. Sprinkle with mixture of garlic salt, onion salt and celery salt. Mix Worcestershire sauce with butter. Drizzle over mixture; toss to mix. Bake at 225 degrees for 1 hour, stirring every 15 minutes. **Yield:** 12 servings.

MUNCHY FUN

Cajun Party Mix

¼ cup margarine
1 tablespoon parsley flakes
1 teaspoon celery salt
1 teaspoon garlic powder
½ teaspoon cayenne pepper
4 to 8 drops of Tabasco sauce
8 cups Crispix cereal
1   3-ounce can French-fried onions,
    chopped

Melt margarine in uncovered roasting pan in 250-degree oven. Stir in parsley flakes, celery salt, garlic powder, cayenne pepper and Tabasco sauce. Add cereal; stir until well coated. Bake for 45 minutes, stirring 3 times. Stir in onions. Cool on paper towels. Store in airtight container. **Yield:** 20 servings.

Cheese Twist Party Mix

1   16-ounce package oyster crackers
1   16-ounce package cheese twists
1 envelope Italian salad dressing mix
1 tablespoon dillweed
2 teaspoons lemon pepper
¼ teaspoon red pepper
2 tablespoons parsley flakes
¼ teaspoon garlic powder
½ teaspoon salt
1 cup vegetable oil

Mix crackers and cheese twists in large baking pan. Combine salad dressing mix, seasonings and oil in bowl; mix well. Pour over crackers; mix well. Bake at 350 degrees for 10 minutes or until light brown, stirring frequently. Pour into brown paper bag; shake well. Cool completely. Store in airtight container. **Yield:** 8 cups.

Make your own favorite snack mix by combining a combination of your favorite cereals, miniature crackers and mixed nuts.

Children's Favorite Party Mix

5 cups Cheerios
2 cups pretzel sticks
1 cup goldfish crackers
1/3 cup melted margarine
1 teaspoon celery flakes
4 teaspoons Worcestershire sauce
1 teaspoon onion powder
1/2 teaspoon garlic powder
1 cup peanuts

Combine Cheerios, pretzel sticks and goldfish crackers in large bowl. Combine margarine, celery flakes, Worcestershire sauce, onion powder and garlic powder in small bowl; mix well. Pour over pretzel mixture; toss to mix. Mix in peanuts. Pour into shallow roasting pan. Bake at 275 degrees for 1 hour, stirring every 10 minutes. Let stand until cool. Store party mix in airtight container. May substitute assorted dry cereals such as wheat squares and rice squares in desired proportions for Cheerios or substitute oyster crackers for goldfish crackers. **Yield:** 16 servings.

Beary Special Snack Mix

3 cups cinnamon toast cereal
2 cups chocolate bear-shaped graham
    snacks
2 cups peanuts
1 1/2 cups "M & M's" Plain Chocolate
    Candies

Mix cereal, snacks, peanuts and candies in large bowl. Store in airtight container. **Yield:** 18 servings.

 Make your child some Zoo Mix by combining Crispie Critters cereal, tinted miniature marshmallows and goldfish crackers.

MUNCHY FUN

MUNCHY FUN

Danish Pecans

3½ cups pecan halves
½ cup melted butter
2 egg whites
Dash of salt
1 cup sugar
¼ teaspoon cinnamon

Spread pecans in 10x15-inch baking pan.
Bake at 325 degrees until lightly toasted.
Remove to plate. Let stand until cool.
Spread melted butter in baking pan. Beat
egg whites with salt, sugar and cinnamon in mixer bowl until stiff peaks
form. Add cooled pecans. Spread in
prepared pan. Bake for 30 minutes, stirring twice. **Yield:** 28 servings.

Spiced Pecans

1 egg white
¼ teaspoon each cinnamon, cloves and
    allspice
½ teaspoon salt
½ cup sugar
2 tablespoons water
4 cups pecan halves

Combine egg white, cinnamon, cloves,
allspice, salt, sugar and water in bowl;
mix well. Let stand for 15 minutes. Stir
in pecan halves. Spread on two 10x15-
inch baking sheets. Bake at 250 degrees
for 1 hour. Remove to waxed paper to
cool. **Yield:** 8 servings.

Sugar-Glazed Walnuts

½ cup butter or margarine
1 cup packed brown sugar
1 teaspoon cinnamon
4 cups walnut halves

Microwave butter in microwave-safe
bowl on High for 1 minute. Stir in brown
sugar and cinnamon. Microwave on
High for 2 minutes. Stir in walnuts.
Microwave for 3 to 5 minutes longer or
until walnuts are evenly glazed. Cool
before serving. **Yield:** 10 servings.

Harvest Popcorn

2 quarts popped popcorn
2 cups canned shoestring potatoes
1 cup mixed nuts
1/3 cup melted butter
1 teaspoon dill
1 teaspoon lemon pepper
1 teaspoon Worcestershire sauce
1/2 teaspoon garlic powder
1/4 teaspoon salt
1/2 teaspoon onion powder

Combine popcorn, potatoes and nuts in large bowl; toss lightly. Combine butter, dill, lemon pepper, Worcestershire sauce, garlic powder, salt and onion powder in small bowl; mix well. Drizzle over popcorn mixture; toss to coat. Serve immediately. **Yield:** 12 servings.

Onion Pretzels

1   18-ounce package pretzels
1 cup margarine
1 envelope onion soup mix

Break pretzels into bite-sized pieces. Melt margarine in 4-quart saucepan. Add soup mix; mix well. Add pretzels gradually, stirring to coat well. Spread on 10x15-inch baking sheet. Bake at 225 degrees for 45 minutes, stirring every 15 minutes. **Yield:** 10 servings.

Spiced Pretzels

1 pound pretzels, broken into pieces
2/3 cup oil
1 envelope ranch salad dressing mix
1/4 teaspoon dillweed
1/2 teaspoon garlic salt

Place pretzels in microwave-safe dish. Combine oil, dressing mix, dillweed and garlic salt in small bowl; mix well. Pour over pretzels, tossing to coat. Microwave on High for 6 minutes, stirring every 2 minutes. Cool and store in airtight container. **Yield:** 8 servings.

MUNCHY FUN

FUN! FUN! FUN!

"Eat and play at the same time. What could be better?"

* Visit a doughnut shop. Watch how they make and fill the pastries, and then take home one of each.

* Play checkers with "M & M's" Chocolate Candies. Use the red and brown pieces for checkers and eat the rest!

* Make a recipe of edible play dough by mixing 1 cup nonfat dry milk powder, 1 cup peanut butter and 1/2 cup honey. Play with half and eat half.

* Make up your own snack mix. Combine your favorite cereals, nuts, candies, chips or other snacks for a one-of-a-kind treat.

* Melt 3 cups chocolate chips with 1 tablespoon oil in double boiler. Use to dip almost any snack such as peanut butter-filled crackers, tiny crackers, pretzels, nuts, marshmallows, dried or frozen fruit or cereal.

* Spread ice cream, sherbet or frozen yogurt between graham crackers or large unfilled cookies for instant ice cream sandwiches. Insert a popsicle stick to make icy lollipops.

GARDEN PATCH FUN

Easy Preserving

Tangy
Uncooked Relish

1 pound ripe tomatoes, chopped
16 small white onions, chopped
4 medium green bell peppers,
 chopped
2 cups seedless golden raisins
1 tablespoon salt
2 cups canned applesauce
2 teaspoons dry mustard
2 cups white vinegar

Combine chopped vegetables, raisins, salt, applesauce and dry mustard in large bowl. Add vinegar; mix well. Spoon into large jar; cover tightly. Refrigerate for 1 week or longer for maximum flavor.
Yield: 2¹/₂ quarts.

Jezebel Sauce

1   10-ounce jar apple jelly
1   10-ounce jar apricot preserves
1   6-ounce jar cream-style
   horseradish
¹/₂   1¹/₂-ounce can dry mustard
1 teaspoon pepper

Combine apple jelly, apricot preserves, horseradish, dry mustard and pepper in saucepan. Bring to a boil, stirring constantly. Cool. Pour mixture into decorative jars; seal. Store jars in refrigerator. Serve over cream cheese as spread or as relish for ham or pork.
Yield: 3 cups.

Slow Cooker Apple Butter

4 pounds Golden Delicious apples,
  peeled
2 cups apple cider
2 teaspoons cinnamon
1 teaspoon cloves
1/8 teaspoon allspice
3 cups sugar

Cut apples into quarters. Combine with cider in slow cooker. Cook on Low for 10 hours. Add cinnamon, cloves, allspice and sugar; mix well. Cook, uncovered, on High for 3 hours or until thickened, stirring occasionally. Spoon into sterilized jars, leaving 1/2 inch headspace. Seal with 2-piece lids. Store in refrigerator. **Yield:** 4 pints.

Processor Apricot-Pineapple Jam

2   6-ounce packages dried apricots
2   16-ounce cans crushed pineapple,
    drained
Juice of 1/2 lemon
1/3 teaspoon grated lemon rind
4 cups sugar

Combine apricots with water to cover in bowl. Let stand overnight. Place undrained apricots in large saucepan. Cook, covered, until apricots are tender. Remove cooked apricots to food processor container with slotted spoon. Pulse 6 times to chop well. Return to hot liquid. Add pineapple, lemon juice, lemon rind and sugar. Simmer until sugar is dissolved, stirring frequently. Cook over high heat for 30 minutes or until thickened to desired consistency. Spoon into hot sterilized jars leaving 1/2 inch headspace. Seal with 2-piece lids. Process in hot water bath for 10 minutes. **Yield:** 3 to 4 pints.

GARDEN PATCH FUN

Ten-Minute Spiced Blueberry Jam

6 cups blueberries, crushed
2 tablespoons lemon juice
7 cups sugar
1 pouch Certo
1/2 teaspoon cinnamon
1/2 teaspoon ground cloves

Combine 4 1/2 cups crushed blueberries and lemon juice in large saucepan. Add sugar. Stir to mix well. Bring to a full rolling boil, stirring constantly. Cook for 1 minute, stirring constantly. Remove from heat. Stir in Certo; skim foam. Stir in cinnamon and cloves. Pour into hot sterilized jars, leaving 1/8 inch headspace. Seal with 2-piece lids. Process in boiling water bath for 5 minutes. **Yield:** 8 cups.

Cherry-Zucchini Jam

1 large zucchini
1/2 cup fresh lemon juice
1   20-ounce can crushed pineapple
6 cups sugar
1   3-ounce package cherry gelatin

Peel and shred zucchini. Combine with lemon juice in saucepan. Simmer for 30 minutes. Stir in pineapple and sugar. Bring to a boil, stirring to dissolve sugar. Cook for 5 minutes; remove from heat. Stir in gelatin until dissolved. Ladle into hot sterilized jars leaving 1/2 inch headspace. Seal with 2-piece lids. Process in boiling water bath for 5 minutes. **Yield:** 2 pints.

Fresh Kiwifruit Jam

1 pound kiwifruit, peeled
2 1/2 cups sugar
1 tablespoon lemon juice
1   3-ounce envelope liquid pectin

Purée kiwifruit in blender. Pour into bowl. Add sugar and lemon juice; stir until sugar dissolves. Let stand, covered, for 20 minutes. Add pectin. Stir for 2 minutes. Let stand, covered, for 24 hours. Pour into 6-ounce jars; seal with 2-piece lids. Store in refrigerator for up to 5 weeks or in freezer for up to 1 year. **Yield:** six to eight 6-ounce jars.

Strawberry and Raspberry Jam

2   10-ounce packages frozen
    strawberries
1   10-ounce package frozen red
    raspberries
5 cups sugar
3/4 cup water
1/2 pouch Certo

Thaw strawberries and raspberries in large saucepan. Add sugar; mix well. Let stand until sugar dissolves. Add water. Bring to a boil, stirring constantly. Cook for 1 minute. Remove from heat. Stir in Certo; skim foam. Pour into hot sterilized jars, leaving 1/8 inch headspace. Seal with 2-piece lids. Process in boiling water bath for 5 minutes. **Yield:** 5 cups.

Grape Freezer Jelly

2   6-ounce cans frozen grape juice
    concentrate, thawed
5 cups sugar
13/4 cups lemon-lime soda
3/4 cup water
1 envelope pectin

Combine grape juice concentrate and sugar in bowl; mix well. Stir in lemon-lime soda. Bring water and pectin to a boil in saucepan, stirring constantly. Stir hot mixture into grape juice mixture. Stir for 3 minutes. Ladle into small 1-pint freezer containers; seal. Let stand at room temperature for 24 hours. Store in freezer. **Yield:** 52/3 pints.

Zucchini Marmalade

6 cups shredded zucchini
41/2 cups sugar
1   20-ounce can crushed pineapple
1/2 cup lemon juice
2   3-ounce packages strawberry gelatin

Combine zucchini with a small amount of water in saucepan. Cook for 6 minutes; drain well. Add sugar, pineapple and lemon juice. Cook for 3 minutes, stirring frequently. Stir in gelatin until dissolved. Spoon into hot sterilized jars, leaving 1/2 inch headspace. Seal with 2-piece lids. **Yield:** 4 pints.

GARDEN PATCH FUN

Peachy Berry Jam

1   10-ounce package frozen sweetened
    strawberries, thawed
1 cup drained canned peaches
1/2 teaspoon ascorbic acid
1/2 cup water
1 package powdered pectin
3 cups sugar
1/4 cup water
1/4 cup slivered almonds
1 tablespoon grated lemon rind

Combine strawberries and peaches in
bowl. Sprinkle fruit with ascorbic acid.
Let stand for 20 minutes. Combine with
1/2 cup water and pectin in saucepan.
Bring to a boil, stirring constantly. Boil
for 1 minute, stirring constantly. Remove
from heat. Add sugar and 1/4 cup water;
mix well. Stir in almonds and lemon
rind. Ladle into hot sterilized jars, leaving 1/2 inch headspace. Seal with 2-piece
lids. Let stand at room temperature for
24 hours. Store in refrigerator.
Yield: 2 pints.

Microwave Pepper
and Honey Jelly

2   4-ounce cans jalapeño peppers,
    finely chopped
1 cup white vinegar
2   2-pound jars light honey
1   3-ounce package liquid pectin

Simmer peppers and vinegar in large
saucepan for 10 minutes. Microwave
honey on High for 1 minute. Add to peppers; mix well. Bring to a boil. Stir in
pectin. Boil for 3 minutes, stirring frequently. Remove from heat; skim. Ladle
into hot sterilized jars, leaving 1/2 inch
headspace. Seal with 2-piece lids or
paraffin. **Yield:** 4 pints.

 *For Freezer Cantaloupe, dissolve
3 cups sugar in 2 cups cold
water. Chill in refrigerator. Add
6 cups cantaloupe balls. Spoon
into freezer containers. Store
in freezer.*

Pepper Jelly to the Third Power

1 large green bell pepper
1 large red bell pepper
2 small banana peppers
3/4 cup tarragon vinegar
1 cup cider
4 cups sugar
3   3-ounce packages liquid pectin

Chop green and red bell peppers very finely. Measure 2 cups. Chop banana peppers very finely. Measure 1/3 cup. Bring peppers and vinegar to a boil in 4-quart saucepan; reduce heat. Simmer for 5 minutes. Add cider and sugar, stirring until sugar is dissolved. Bring to a full rolling boil, stirring constantly. Cook for 1 minute, stirring constantly. Stir in 1 package pectin. Boil for 1 minute, stirring constantly. Remove from heat. Stir in remaining pectin. Let stand for 20 minutes, stirring occasionally. Ladle into hot sterilized jars, leaving 1/2 inch headspace. Seal with 2-piece lids.
Yield: 4 3/4 cups.

Easy Pepper Medley

10 green bell peppers
6 red bell peppers
6 yellow bell peppers
1/4 cup corn oil
4 teaspoons salt
2 cups water
2 cups cider vinegar
1 1/2 cups sugar

Discard stems, seed and membrane of bell peppers; cut into quarters. Place in large saucepan. Add water to cover. Bring to a boil, stirring occasionally; reduce heat. Simmer for 4 minutes; drain. Pack into hot sterilized 1-pint jars. Add 1 1/2 teaspoons oil and 1/2 teaspoon salt to each jar. Combine 2 cups water, vinegar and sugar in saucepan. Bring to a boil, stirring until sugar dissolves. Pour over bell peppers in jars, leaving 1/2 inch headspace; seal with 2-piece lids. Process in boiling water bath for 10 minutes.
Yield: eight 1-pint jars.

Quick Apple-Pepper Relish

12 large apples, cored
6 red bell peppers, seeded
6 green bell peppers, seeded
4 large onions, peeled
3 hot peppers
2 cups apple cider vinegar
1 cup packed light brown sugar
5 cups sugar
1 cup prepared mustard

Force unpeeled apples, red and green peppers, onions and hot peppers through food grinder. Mix vinegar, brown sugar, sugar and mustard in large saucepan. Bring to a boil, stirring frequently. Simmer for 5 minutes, stirring frequently. Ladle into hot sterilized 1-pint jars, leaving ½ inch headspace. Seal with 2-piece lids. Serve with cream cheese and crackers or as an accompaniment with meat or beans. **Yield:** 13 pints.

Cool-in-the-Kitchen Fruit Salsa

1 green bell pepper, chopped
1 yellow bell pepper, chopped
1 red bell pepper, chopped
Minced jalapeño pepper to taste
1 papaya or mango, chopped
1 pineapple, peeled, chopped
½ cup finely chopped cilantro
1 purple onion, chopped

Combine bell peppers, jalapeño pepper, papaya or mango, pineapple, cilantro and onion in bowl; mix well. Ladle into hot sterilized 1-pint jars. Store in refrigerator. Serve as dip with corn chips or as an accompaniment with grilled fish or chicken. **Yield:** 3 to 4 pints.

Freezer Slaw

1 medium head cabbage, shredded
1 teaspoon salt
1 cup vinegar
1/4 cup water
2 cups sugar
1 teaspoon celery seed
1 teaspoon mustard seed
1 medium carrot, grated
1 medium green bell pepper, finely
chopped

Mix cabbage and salt in large bowl. Let stand for 1 hour. Combine vinegar, water, sugar, celery seed and mustard seed in small saucepan. Bring to a boil. Cook for 1 minute, stirring to mix well. Cool to lukewarm. Press moisture from cabbage mixture. Add carrot and green pepper; mix well. Add lukewarm dressing; mix well. Spoon into freezer containers, leaving 1/2 inch headspace. Freeze until needed. **Yield:** 8 servings.

Speedy Squashickles

8 cups sliced yellow squash
2 cups sliced onions
3 green bell peppers, cut into strips
2 tablespoons salt
3 cups sugar
2 cups vinegar
2 teaspoons mustard seed
2 teaspoons celery seed

Combine squash, onions and green peppers in large bowl. Sprinkle with salt. Let stand for 1 hour; drain. Combine sugar, vinegar, mustard seed and celery seed in large saucepan. Bring to a boil, stirring until sugar dissolves; remove from heat. Add vegetables; mix gently. Ladle into hot sterilized 1-pint jars, leaving 1/4 inch headspace; seal with 2-piece lids. Process in boiling water bath for 10 minutes. **Yield:** 5 pints.

GARDEN PATCH FUN

FUN! FUN! FUN!

"Have fun with bounty from your garden—or the grocery."

* Make "food print" gift wrap by dipping cut apples, pears, oranges or lemons in acrylic paint and printing on heavy brown or white paper.

* Make a summer wreath using firm vegetables like peppers, squash, broccoli, cauliflower, etc. Hang the wreath in the kitchen or use as a centerpiece with a fat candle in the center.

* Plant an indoor garden with leftovers. Sweet potatoes or carrot tops grow pretty greenery in shallow dishes of water.

* Serve dinner in vegetable containers: hollowed out bell peppers, cabbages, squash, tomatoes or cucumbers.

* Create veggie people for fun or for decoration. Add edible faces— potato slice ears, radish eyes, pepper noses, cucumber slice mouths and parsley hair—to potatoes, squash or pumpkins. Use toothpicks for fasteners.

* Serve dessert in a flowerpot. Place cookies in the bottom of small, new, washed flowerpots. Fill with layers of pudding or ice cream, toppings and whipped topping. Decorate with fresh flower placed in straw inserted in dessert. Garnish with gummy worms.

COOK-OUT FUN

Grill
Specialties

Spanish Pepper Chicken

1 tablespoon peppercorns
1½ cups pimento-stuffed olives
1 clove of garlic
½ teaspoon grated lemon rind
¼ cup olive oil
3½ pounds broiler-fryer chicken
    pieces

Whirl peppercorns in blender container until crushed. Add olives, garlic, lemon rind and olive oil; blend until thick and fairly smooth. Spread olive mixture over chicken; place in shallow dish. Chill for 2 hours. Grill chicken on both sides 6 inches from hot coals for 35 to 40 minutes or until tender. **Yield**: 6 servings.

Picnic Tea

1 cup water
2 tea bags
¼ 12-ounce can frozen cranberry
    juice concentrate
1 6 ounce can frozen orange juice
    concentrate
½ cup pear nectar

Bring water to a boil in saucepan. Add tea bags; remove from heat. Let stand, covered, for 5 minutes. Remove tea bags. Add juice concentrates and pear nectar. Stir until concentrates melt. Serve over ice. **Yield:** 2½ cups.

Summertime Beef Kabobs

1 cup oil
1/4 cup soy sauce
1/4 cup Worcestershire sauce
1/4 cup Dijon mustard
1/4 cup fresh lemon juice
2 large cloves of garlic, crushed
1 to 2 teaspoons coarsely ground pepper
1   5-pound sirloin tip roast
2 Bermuda onions
1 green bell pepper
1 red bell pepper
1 yellow bell pepper
1 pound new potatoes
1 pound mushrooms
2 pints cherry tomatoes

Combine oil, soy sauce, Worcestershire sauce, mustard, lemon juice, garlic and pepper in bowl; mix well. Cut beef into 1½-inch cubes. Add to marinade, turning to coat well. Marinate in refrigerator for 24 hours, stirring occasionally. Cut onions and bell peppers into large chunks. Parboil new potatoes; drain. Drain beef, reserving marinade. Thread beef alternately with vegetables onto skewers. Grill over hot coals for 3 minutes on each side, basting frequently with reserved marinade.
Yield: 10 servings.

Grilled Flank Steak

3/4 cup corn oil
1/4 cup soy sauce
2 tablespoons Worcestershire sauce
1 tablespoon dry mustard
1⅛ teaspoons salt
1½ teaspoons pepper
2 tablespoons wine vinegar
1⅛ teaspoons parsley flakes
1 clove of garlic, crushed
1/3 cup lemon juice
3 pounds flank steak

Combine oil, soy sauce, Worcestershire sauce, mustard, salt, pepper, vinegar, parsley, garlic and lemon juice in shallow bowl; mix well. Add flank steak. Marinate for several hours, turning occasionally. Grill over hot coals until of desired degree of doneness. Slice diagonally to serve. **Yield:** 8 servings.

Spicy Steak

¼ to ½ cup melted butter
1   3-pound sirloin steak
1 tablespoon garlic powder
1 tablespoon onion powder
1 tablespoon chili powder
1 tablespoon salt
1 tablespoon ground cumin
1 tablespoon oregano
1 tablespoon paprika
1 tablespoon black pepper
¼ to ½ teaspoon cayenne pepper
Spicy Mayonnaise
6 pita breads, split
Tomato Topping
½ head lettuce, shredded

Pour melted butter into shallow flat dish. Add steak, turning to coat. Combine garlic powder, onion powder, chili powder, salt, cumin, oregano, paprika, black pepper and cayenne pepper in small bowl; mix well. Sprinkle over steak, coating thickly. Grill steak over hot coals to desired degree of doneness. Let stand for 10 minutes. Slice very thin. Combine with Spicy Mayonnaise in bowl; stir to coat. Spoon into pita pockets. Top with Tomato Topping and lettuce.
Yield: 6 servings.

Spicy Mayonnaise

1 cup mayonnaise
½ teaspoon cayenne pepper
1 jalapeño pepper, chopped

Combine mayonnaise, cayenne pepper and jalapeño pepper in small bowl; mix well. Chill in refrigerator until serving time. **Yield:** 1 cup.

Tomato Topping

2 to 3 medium tomatoes, chopped
¼ cup minced onion
½ teaspoon minced garlic
¼ teaspoon salt
¼ teaspoon pepper
1 tablespoon minced parsley
⅛ teaspoon sugar

Combine tomatoes, onion, garlic, salt, pepper, parsley and sugar in bowl; mix well. **Yield:** 2 cups.

Outdoor Tenderloin

1   3-pound beef tenderloin
Garlic salt to taste
Pepper to taste
3 tablespoons brown sugar
3 tablespoons Dijon mustard
8 ounces bacon

Sprinkle beef with garlic salt, pepper and brown sugar. Spread with mustard. Arrange bacon in crisscross pattern over beef; secure with wooden picks. Prepare 25 to 30 coals on each side of grill. Place beef on sheet of foil in center of grill; close grill. Grill for 1 hour.
Yield: 8 servings.

Oriental Pork Chops

$1/3$ cup soy sauce
$1/4$ cup oil
$1/4$ cup orange juice
$1/4$ cup chopped green bell pepper
1 tablespoon brown sugar
2 teaspoons ginger
1 teaspoon turmeric
6   $1^1/2$-inch pork chops

Combine soy sauce, oil, orange juice, green pepper, brown sugar, ginger and turmeric in bowl; mix well. Arrange pork chops in shallow dish. Add marinade. Marinate, covered, in refrigerator for 3 hours to overnight, turning occasionally. Drain, reserving marinade. Place pork chops on grill over low coals and hickory chips. Grill for 25 minutes on each side, basting occasionally with reserved marinade. **Yield:** 6 servings.

Wonderful Ribs

20 pounds ranch-style pork ribs
Tabasco sauce to taste
2   16-ounce bottles of spicy barbecue
    sauce

Cut ribs into 4-inch serving pieces. Arrange in pressure cooker, filling halfway. Pressure cook using manufacturer's instructions for 8 to 9 minutes. Remove from pressure cooker. Coat with mixture of Tabasco sauce and barbecue sauce. Chill in refrigerator. Cook on grill or smoker over low coals until light brown. Coat well with sauce. **Yield:** 20 servings.

COOK-OUT FUN

Barbecued Chicken

1 egg, beaten
1 cup oil
2 cups cider vinegar
1 tablespoon poultry seasoning
3 tablespoons salt
1 tablespoon pepper
8 pieces of chicken

Beat egg and oil in bowl until smooth. Stir in vinegar, poultry seasoning, salt and pepper. Rinse chicken and pat dry. Add to marinade. Marinate, covered, overnight, turning occasionally. Drain, reserving marinade. Grill over hot coals until tender, basting with reserved marinade. **Yield:** 8 servings.

Great Grilled Chicken

10 pieces of chicken
1 cup mayonnaise
1½ cups Italian salad dressing
½ cup lemon juice
¼ cup soy sauce
¼ teaspoon Tabasco sauce
2 teaspoons Worcestershire sauce

Rinse chicken and pat dry. Arrange in shallow baking dish. Bake at 325 degrees for 30 minutes or microwave on Medium for 15 to 20 minutes. Combine mayonnaise, salad dressing, lemon juice, soy sauce, Tabasco sauce and Worcestershire sauce in bowl; mix well. Place chicken on grill over low coals. Grill for 20 minutes or until brown, basting with mayonnaise sauce. **Yield:** 10 servings.

Pepper Jelly Chicken

4 chicken breasts
⅓ cup hot pepper jelly
⅓ cup apple juice

Rinse chicken breasts and pat dry. Place skin side down over hot coals on grill. Grill for 15 minutes or until chicken is brown; turn chicken. Brush with mixture of jelly and apple juice. Grill until brown; turn. Brush with jelly mixture. Grill until chicken is tender, dark brown and crisp, turning and brushing occasionally with jelly mixture. Heat any remaining jelly mixture. Serve with chicken.
Yield: 4 servings.

Grilled Turkey Tenderloin

1/4 cup soy sauce
1/4 cup oil
2 tablespoons lemon juice
1/4 cup dry cooking sherry
2 tablespoons onion flakes
1/4 teaspoon ginger
Garlic salt to taste
Pepper to taste
1 pound turkey tenderloins, 3/4 to 1
    inch thick

Combine soy sauce, oil, lemon juice, sherry, onion flakes, ginger, garlic salt and pepper in shallow dish; mix well. Rinse turkey and pat dry. Add to marinade, turning to coat well. Marinate, covered, in refrigerator for several hours, turning occasionally; drain. Grill over hot coals for 6 to 8 minutes on each side or until no longer pink in center; do not overcook. **Yield:** 4 servings.

Marinated Fish Filets

2 tablespoons soy sauce
1 clove of garlic, minced
1/3 cup catsup
2 tablespoons lemon juice
1 teaspoon oregano
1/2 cup orange juice
1 tablespoon parsley
4 pollack or halibut filets

Combine soy sauce, garlic, catsup, lemon juice, oregano, orange juice and parsley in sealable bag. Add fish. Marinate for 30 minutes or longer; drain. Grill fish over hot coals until fish flakes easily. **Yield:** 4 servings.

Cajun Spice Mix

1 tablespoon paprika
2 teaspoons salt
1 teaspoon each onion powder, garlic
    powder and cayenne pepper
3/4 teaspoon each white pepper and
    black pepper
1/2 teaspoon each thyme and oregano

Combine all spices in shaker container. Shake well to mix. Sprinkle over chicken or fish for grilling. **Yield:** 10 1/2 teaspoons.

COOK-OUT FUN

COOK-OUT FUN

Stuffed Flounder

1 package Stove-Top stuffing
1/2 cup chopped onion
1/2 cup chopped celery
2 tablespoons melted margarine
1/2 cup chopped crab meat or shrimp
2   12-inch whole flounder
2 slices bacon
Salt and pepper to taste

Prepare stuffing using package directions. Sauté onion and celery in margarine in skillet. Stir into stuffing. Add crab meat; mix well. Slit dark side of flounder to create pocket for stuffing. Stuff with stuffing mixture. Place on foiled-lined gas grill. Top with bacon. Season with salt and pepper. Grill for 20 to 30 minutes or until fish flakes easily. **Yield:** 4 servings.

Italian Grilled Orange Roughy

4 orange roughy filets
1   8-ounce bottle of Italian salad
    dressing

Marinate fish in salad dressing in shallow dish for 30 minutes; drain. Grill fish over hot coals for 8 minutes or until fish flakes easily, basting with dressing occasionally. Serve with hot cooked rice or buttered noodles. **Yield:** 4 servings.

Bacon-Stuffed Trout

2 eggs
1 tablespoon milk
1 teaspoon parsley flakes
1 clove of garlic, minced
1/2 teaspoon allspice
8 medium trout
8 to 16 slices grilled bacon

Combine eggs, milk, parsley, garlic and allspice in bowl; beat well. Coat fish inside and out with egg mixture. Place 1 or 2 bacon slices in each trout. Place trout on hot greased grill. Grill over hot coals for 20 minutes or until fish flakes easily, turning once. **Yield:** 8 servings.

Banana-Dijon Grilled Shrimp

^{1}/$_2$ cup mashed ripe banana
^{1}/$_4$ cup reduced-calorie mayonnaise
1 tablespoon lime juice
1 tablespoon Dijon mustard
1 tablespoon honey
1 teaspoon grated lime rind
^{1}/$_4$ teaspoon ground red pepper
1 cup plain nonfat yogurt
1^1/$_2$ pounds large unpeeled shrimp

Combine banana, mayonnaise, lime juice, mustard, honey, lime rind and red pepper in food processor container. Process at High speed for 5 seconds. Scrape sides with rubber spatula. Process for 5 seconds longer or until smooth. Pour into bowl; stir in yogurt. Spoon 1 cup banana sauce into shallow flat dish. Cover and chill remaining sauce. Peel and devein shrimp, leaving tails. Thread 6 shrimp onto eight 10-inch skewers. Place in banana sauce. Spray grill rack with nonstick cooking spray. Grill shrimp over medium hot coals for 4 minutes on each side. Serve with chilled banana sauce. **Yield:** 4 servings.

Grilled Stuffed Mushrooms

8 large whole mushrooms
2 tablespoons fresh bread crumbs
1 green onion, finely chopped
1 tomato, peeled, chopped
1 teaspoon tomato paste
1 teaspoon lemon juice
^{1}/$_2$ teaspoon dried thyme
^{1}/$_4$ teaspoon dried oregano
Salt and pepper to taste

Remove mushroom caps and set aside. Chop stems finely. Combine with bread crumbs, green onion, tomato, tomato paste, lemon juice, thyme, oregano, salt and pepper in small bowl; mix well. Spoon mixture into mushroom caps. Butter double thickness of heavy-duty foil on shiny side. Arrange mushrooms on foil; fold up, securing edges. Grill over medium-hot coals for 5 to 6 minutes. **Yield:** 8 servings.

Grilled Herb Potatoes

2 medium onions
6 medium potatoes
3/4 cup margarine
1/4 cup finely chopped celery
1 teaspoon crushed dried oregano
1/2 teaspoon salt
1/4 teaspoon garlic powder
1/8 teaspoon pepper

Slice onions thinly; cut into halves crosswise. Cut potatoes into 1/2-inch slices, cutting to but not through bottom. Place on pieces of foil. Sauté celery in margarine in skillet until tender. Stir in oregano, salt, garlic powder and pepper. Drizzle half the mixture into slices in potatoes. Insert onion slices. Drizzle with remaining celery mixture. Wrap potatoes in foil; seal securely with double fold. Grill over hot coals for 40 to 45 minutes or until tender. **Yield:** 6 servings.

Grilled Zucchini

8 zucchini, sliced lengthwise
3 tablespoons oil
1 1/2 teaspoons basil

Brush zucchini in shallow dish with mixture of oil and basil. Marinate in refrigerator for 2 hours. Grill over low heat coals until tender, turning frequently. **Yield:** 8 servings.

Vegetable Care Packages

12 ounces fresh or frozen peas
8 ounces fresh whole kernel corn
1 green bell pepper, finely chopped
1 red bell pepper, finely chopped
1/4 cup butter
1 teaspoon tarragon
Salt and pepper to taste

Cut heavy-duty foil into four 6x6-inch squares. Layer each square with an equal portion of peas, corn, green pepper and red pepper. Dot each layer with 1 tablespoon butter, 1/4 teaspoon tarragon, salt and pepper. Wrap tightly in foil. Grill over medium-hot coals for 20 to 30 minutes. **Yield:** 4 servings.

Barbecued Apples

4 small Granny Smith apples
1/4 cup packed dark brown sugar
2 tablespoons raisins
1 teaspoon grated lemon rind
1/2 teaspoon cinnamon

Core and cut ring around each apple
with knife. Mix brown sugar, raisins,
lemon rind and cinnamon in small bowl.
Spoon mixture into cored centers. Wrap
each apple in heavy-duty foil with shiny
side against the apple. Grill over warm
coals for 40 minutes, turning occasionally. Unwrap carefully to serve.
Yield: 4 servings.

Grilled Pear and Banana Kabobs

2 pears, peeled, cut into chunks
2 bananas, peeled, cut into chunks
16 large strawberries, hulled
Juice of 2 lemons
3 tablespoons sugar

Combine fruit in bowl. Sprinkle with
lemon juice and 1 1/2 tablespoons sugar.
Let stand for 30 minutes. Thread onto
skewers; coat with remaining sugar. Grill
over medium coals for 5 to 6 minutes or
until sugar caramelizes.
Yield: 4 servings.

Parsley-Cheese French Bread

1   16-ounce loaf French bread
2 to 3 cups shredded sharp Cheddar
   cheese
1/2 cup finely chopped parsley
1 tablespoon (about) Worcestershire
   sauce
1/2 cup (or more) mayonnaise
Garlic powder to taste
Salt and pepper to taste

Cut bread into slices to but not through
bottom. Combine Cheddar cheese,
parsley, Worcestershire sauce, mayonnaise, garlic powder, salt and pepper in
bowl; mix well. Spread slices with cheese
mixture. Wrap loaf tightly in foil. Grill
over medium hot coals, turning often.
Yield: 15 servings.

FUN! FUN! FUN!

"Work up an appetite while the coals are heating and the food is cooking."

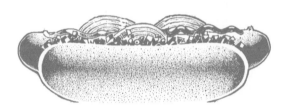

COOK-OUT FUN

* Make a giant outdoor ice bucket. Fill a wheelbarrow or wagon with ice and chill soft drinks.

* Fill the sky with flying kites.

* Catch lightening bugs and let them go.

* Use plastic garbage bags for everything—to marinate the roast; to toss a huge salad; to make puppy chow for dessert. When the eating's over, use the bags to clean up (recycling, of course).

* Play a rousing game of Kick the Can, Duck Duck Goose, Red Rover, Dodge Ball, Volleyball, etc.

* Play a cool game of Statues, Freeze Tag, Hide and Seek or Croquet.

* Swing.

PICNIC
FUN

Portable
Treats

Cyclers Sub

1½ cups finely chopped cabbage
½ cup shredded Swiss cheese
¼ cup shredded carrots
2 tablespoons finely chopped parsley
2 tablespoons chopped green bell
   pepper
1 tablespoon finely chopped pimento
1 tablespoon fresh lemon juice
1 tablespoon creamy French
   salad dressing
1 teaspoon grated onion
½ teaspoon celery salt
¼ teaspoon dry mustard
¼ teaspoon salt
3 French rolls, split
¼ cup butter, softened
1 tablespoon prepared mustard
6 ounces thinly sliced salami
8 ounces Cheddar cheese, sliced
3 dill pickle sticks or slices

Combine cabbage, Swiss cheese, carrots, parsley, green pepper, pimento, lemon juice, salad dressing, onion, celery salt, dry mustard and salt in bowl; toss lightly. Hollow out the centers of rolls. Spread mixture of butter and prepared mustard over inside of roll halves. Layer salami, Cheddar cheese and coleslaw mixture over roll halves. Top with a pickle stick in the center of bottom half of roll. Place top and bottom half of roll side by side and roll together. Chill, wrapped, for several hours.
Yield: 6 servings.

Fruit Dip

8 ounces cream cheese, softened
2 tablespoons orange juice
¼ cup confectioners' sugar
1   7-ounce jar marshmallow creme

Combine first 3 ingredients in bowl; mix until smooth. Fold in marshmallow creme. Serve with bite-sized fruit for dippers. **Yield:** 8 servings.

Pretzel Dip

1   8-ounce bottle of ranch salad
     dressing
½ cup (or more) prepared mustard

Blend salad dressing and mustard in serving bowl. Chill until serving time. Serve with pretzels. **Yield:** 6 servings.

Sausage Balls

1 pound Cheddar cheese
1 pound hot sausage
3 cups baking mix

Melt cheese in double boiler. Combine with sausage in bowl; mix well. Add baking mix; mix well. Shape into balls; place on baking sheet. Bake at 350 degrees for 20 to 25 minutes or until brown. **Yield:** 36 servings.

Vegetable Bars

2   8-count cans crescent rolls
16 ounces cream cheese, softened
½ cup mayonnaise
1 envelope ranch salad dressing mix
½ cup each chopped cauliflower,
     broccoli, carrot, green bell pepper
     and green onions
8 ounces shredded Cheddar cheese

Line 10x15-inch baking pan with dough; press to seal perforations. Bake using package directions. Let stand until cool. Mix cream cheese, mayonnaise and salad dressing mix in bowl until smooth. Spread on baked layer. Mix cauliflower, broccoli, carrot, green pepper and green onions in bowl. Sprinkle over cream cheese layer, pressing lightly. Sprinkle with Cheddar cheese. **Yield:** 48 servings.

Cow Patties

1 pound ground beef
2 potatoes, sliced
1 onion, thinly sliced
Salt and pepper to taste

Shape ground beef into four ½-inch thick patties. Layer half the potato slices, ground beef patties, onion slices and remaining potato slices on heavy-duty foil. Sprinkle with salt and pepper. Seal foil tightly; place on baking sheet. Bake at 300 degrees for 45 to 60 minutes. **Yield:** 4 servings.

Marinated Shrimp

2 quarts water
1 tablespoon salt
Celery tops to taste
2 bay leaves
2 pounds medium shrimp in shells
2 medium red onions, sliced
2 tablespoons capers
1 cup oil
½ cup white vinegar
2 teaspoons celery seed
1 teaspoon salt
Tabasco sauce to taste

Bring water, 1 tablespoon salt, celery tops and bay leaves to a boil in large saucepan. Simmer for 10 minutes. Add shrimp. Return to a boil; remove from heat. Let stand for 5 minutes. Drain shrimp and rinse with cold water. Peel and devein shrimp. Layer shrimp, onions and capers in medium bowl. Pour mixture of remaining ingredients over layers. Marinate, covered, in refrigerator for 8 hours. Drain before serving. **Yield:** 4 servings.

Creamy Bacon Bars

3 ounces cream cheese, softened
4 slices crisp-fried bacon, crumbled
1 tablespoon milk
1 teaspoon horseradish
½ teaspoon Worcestershire sauce
12 slices white bread, crusts trimmed

Combine first 5 ingredients in bowl; mix well. Spread on half the bread slices; top with remaining bread. Cut each sandwich into thirds. **Yield:** 18 servings.

Chicken Croissants

2 cups chopped cooked chicken
1/2 cup pineapple tidbits
1/4 cup chopped celery
1/2 cup mayonnaise-style salad dressing
8 miniature croissants

Combine chicken, pineapple, celery and salad dressing in bowl; mix well. Split croissants. Fill with chicken mixture. Wrap each in plastic wrap. Chill until serving time. **Yield:** 8 servings.

Cucumber Sandwiches

1 cup plain nonfat yogurt
2 teaspoons dry Italian salad dressing mix
1 tablespoon low-fat mayonnaise
30 party rye bread slices
30 thin cucumber slices
30 fresh dill sprigs

Drain yogurt in colander in refrigerator overnight. Combine with salad dressing mix and mayonnaise in small bowl; mix well. Let stand for 30 minutes. Spread on bread slices. Top each with cucumber slice and dill sprig. Chill, covered, until serving time. **Yield:** 30 servings.

Devilish Mini-Sandwiches

2 ounces cream cheese, softened
1   4-ounce can light deviled ham
1/3 cup whole-berry cranberry sauce
32 slices cocktail pumpernickel bread

Combine cream cheese, deviled ham and cranberry sauce in bowl. Chill, covered, for 1 hour. Spread over half the bread slices. Top with remaining slices. **Yield:** 16 servings.

Mix crunchy peanut butter and applesauce for a sandwich filling children will love.

PICNIC FUN

Dried Beef Sandwich Filling

4 ounces dried beef
4 ounces sharp Cheddar cheese
1 medium onion
1 medium green bell pepper
2 eggs, beaten
1 tablespoon flour
1 6-ounce can tomato purée

Grind first 4 ingredients together. Combine with eggs, flour and tomato purée in saucepan. Cook for 10 minutes or until thickened, stirring constantly. Cool to room temperature. Store in refrigerator.
Yield: 20 servings.

Ham Delights

2 packages small brown and serve rolls
8 thin slices Danish ham
8 slices Swiss cheese
¾ cup margarine, softened
¼ cup minced onion
1 tablespoon poppy seed
3 tablespoons prepared mustard

Slice block of rolls into halves horizontally, leaving bottom half in packaged pan. Layer with ham and cheese. Replace top of rolls. Combine margarine, onion, poppy seed and mustard in small bowl; mix well. Spread over top half of rolls.. Bake at 300 degrees for 8 minutes or until light brown. Slice between individual rolls; arrange on serving plate.
Yield: 20 to 24 rolls.

Pecan-Cream Cheese Sandwiches

16 slices white, whole wheat or rye
   bread
¼ cup butter or margarine, softened
8 ounces cream cheese, softened
⅔ cup finely chopped pecans
3 tablespoons finely chopped onion
3 hard-boiled eggs, finely chopped
3 tablespoons chili sauce
3 tablespoons chopped green bell pepper

Spread 1 side of bread slices lightly with butter. Combine remaining ingredients in bowl; mix well. Spread on half the bread slices; top with remaining bread.
Yield: 8 servings.

Picnic Sandwiches

8 ounces cream cheese, softened
3 tablespoons finely chopped onion
3 tablespoons finely chopped green
   bell pepper
2/3 cup finely chopped pecans
3 tablespoons chili sauce
3 hard-boiled eggs, finely chopped
1 large loaf sandwich bread, crusts
   trimmed
Butter or margarine, softened

Combine cream cheese, onion, green
pepper, pecans, chili sauce and eggs in
bowl; mix well. Spread bread lightly
with butter, covering surface completely.
Spread with filling. Cut each slice into
triangles. Store in refrigerator.
Yield: 48 servings.

Ribbon Sandwiches

2 loaves unsliced white bread
2 loaves unsliced whole wheat bread
2 pounds pimento cheese spread
2 pounds ham salad
2 pounds chicken salad
32 ounces cream cheese, softened
Garlic salt and onion salt to taste
Milk

Trim crusts from bread and cut each loaf
into 4 horizontal slices. Spread pimento
cheese on bottom slice of each loaf. Top
with slice of alternating color of bread.
Spread with ham salad; top with slice of
alternating color of bread. Spread with
chicken salad. Top with remaining bread
slices. Combine cream cheese with garlic
salt, onion salt and enough milk to make
of spreading consistency in bowl; mix
until smooth. Spread over loaves. Chill,
wrapped, overnight. Cut into vertical
slices. **Yield:** 50 servings.

Tuna Salad Filling

1   6-ounce can water-pack tuna, drained
1/2 cup chopped unpeeled cucumber
3 tablespoons mayonnaise
1/8 teaspoon onion powder
1/8 teaspoon dry mustard

Combine all ingredients in bowl; mix
well. Chill in refrigerator.
Yield: 4 servings.

PICNIC FUN

Sour Cream-Ham Sandwiches

2 5-ounce cans chunk ham
1 tablespoon (heaping) mayonnaise
1 cup sour cream
1 teaspoon onion juice
36 slices bread

Flake ham into bowl. Stir in mayonnaise, sour cream and onion juice. Trim crusts from bread. Spread half the bread slices lightly with ham mixture; top with remaining bread. **Yield:** 36 sandwiches.

Antipasto Salad

2 8-ounce jars marinated artichoke hearts
1 red onion, sliced
1 green bell pepper, thinly sliced
1 6-ounce can pitted black olives, drained
1 6-ounce jar green olives, drained
1/2 cup olive oil
1/4 cup wine vinegar
1/2 cup sugar
1 tablespoon salt
1/2 teaspoon pepper
2 cups cherry tomatoes
8 ounces fresh mushrooms, sliced

Combine artichokes and marinade with onion, green pepper and olives in bowl; mix well. Add olive oil, vinegar, sugar, salt and pepper. Marinate in refrigerator overnight. Add tomatoes and mushrooms at serving time. **Yield:** 6 servings.

Copper Carrots

3 pounds carrots, sliced
1 onion, chopped
1 green bell pepper, chopped or sliced
3/4 cup vinegar
3/4 cup sugar
1 teaspoon prepared mustard
1 teaspoon Worcestershire sauce
1 10-ounce can cream of tomato soup

Cook carrots in saucepan until tender; cool. Arrange in shallow 2-quart dish. Sprinkle with onion and green pepper. Pour mixture of remaining ingredients over carrots. Chill, covered, for 12 to 24 hours. **Yield:** 8 to 10 servings.

Cauliflower Salad

Flowerets of 1 large head cauliflower
2 medium tomatoes, chopped
8 ounces bacon, crisp-fried, crumbled
1 cup Cheddar cheese cubes
1/2 cup sliced pimento-stuffed olives
1/2 cup drained chopped pimentos

Combine all ingredients in bowl; toss to mix just before serving. **Yield:** 6 servings.

Marinated Coleslaw

2 onions
1 green bell pepper
3 pounds cabbage, shredded
1 cup sugar
1 cup oil
1 cup vinegar
2 cups sugar
2 teaspoons celery salt
1 teaspoon celery seed

Press onions and green pepper through food grinder. Combine onions, green pepper and cabbage in bowl; toss to mix. Sprinkle with 1 cup sugar. Combine oil, vinegar, remaining 2 cups sugar, celery salt and celery seed in saucepan; mix well. Bring to a boil. Pour over cabbage mixture; toss to mix. Chill until serving time. **Yield:** 25 servings.

Four-Bean Salad

1   15-ounce can garbanzo beans
1   15-ounce can kidney beans
1   15-ounce can green beans
1   15-ounce can wax beans
2 stalks celery, chopped
1 red onion, chopped
1   2-ounce can chopped pimento, drained
3/4 cup vinegar
3/4 cup sugar
1 teaspoon salt
1/4 teaspoon pepper

Drain beans. Combine with celery, onion and pimento in large bowl. Combine vinegar, sugar, salt and pepper in small saucepan. Heat until sugar dissolves, stirring frequently. Pour over salad; mix well. Chill for several hours to 2 weeks. **Yield:** 10 servings.

PICNIC FUN

Marinated Green Beans

1/2 cup wine vinegar
1/4 cup water
11/2 tablespoons oil
1/4 teaspoon salt
1/4 teaspoon pepper
1/2 cup sugar
1   16-ounce can whole green beans,
    drained
1 onion, thinly sliced

Combine vinegar, water, oil, salt, pepper and sugar in small bowl; mix well. Layer green beans and onion in glass dish. Pour marinade over top. Marinate, covered, in refrigerator for 24 hours. Drain and discard marinade before serving. **Yield:** 6 to 8 servings.

Pasta Vinaigrette Salad

4 ounces vermicelli or thin spaghetti,
    broken
1/2 cup canola oil
1/4 cup red wine vinegar
1 clove of garlic, minced
1/4 teaspoon basil
1/4 teaspoon salt
1/8 teaspoon pepper
1   6-ounce jar marinated artichokes,
    drained
1 cup sliced mushrooms
2 tomatoes, peeled, chopped
1/4 cup chopped walnuts
2 tablespoons chopped parsley

Cook pasta using package directions. Rinse in cold water; drain. Combine oil, vinegar, garlic, basil, salt and pepper in jar. Shake, covered, until well mixed. Chop artichokes. Combine pasta, artichokes and mushrooms in bowl. Add dressing, tossing to mix. Chill, covered, in refrigerator. Sprinkle with tomatoes, walnuts and parsley just before serving. **Yield:** 8 servings.

Peach Salad

1 21-ounce can peach pie filling
2 bananas, sliced
1 11-ounce can mandarin oranges,
   drained

Combine pie filling, bananas and mandarin oranges in bowl; mix well. Chill until serving time. **Yield:** 8 servings.

Sunny Fruit Salad

1/2 cup plain yogurt
2 teaspoons honey
1 teaspoon fresh lemon juice
Sections of 2 oranges
2 large bananas, cut into 1/2-inch slices
3 kiwifruit, cut into 1/2-inch slices

Combine yogurt, honey and lemon juice in bowl; mix well. Add orange sections, bananas and kiwifruit; toss to mix. **Yield:** 4 servings.

Veggie Salad

1 20-ounce can white Shoe Peg corn,
   drained
1 20-ounce can small green peas,
   drained
1 20-ounce can French-style green
   beans
1 cup finely chopped onions
1 cup finely sliced celery
1 cup finely chopped green bell pepper
1 4-ounce jar chopped pimentos
1/2 cup vegetable oil
1 cup sugar
3/4 cup white vinegar
Salt and pepper to taste

Combine corn, green peas, green beans, onions, celery, green pepper and pimentos in bowl; toss to mix. Combine oil, sugar and vinegar in microwave-safe bowl. Microwave on High for several minutes; stir until sugar is dissolved. Pour over vegetables; mix well. Cool slightly. Chill overnight to several days, stirring once each day. Season with salt and pepper just before serving. **Yield:** 24 servings.

PICNIC FUN

PICNIC FUN

Coconut-Orange Bread

2 cups sifted flour
1/2 cup sugar
2 1/2 teaspoons baking powder
1 teaspoon salt
1 cup flaked coconut, toasted
2 tablespoons grated orange rind
2 eggs, beaten
1 cup milk
1/4 cup oil

Sift flour, sugar, baking powder and salt into large bowl. Add toasted coconut and orange rind; mix well. Beat together eggs, milk and oil in small bowl. Add to flour mixture, stirring until smooth. Pour into greased 5x9-inch loaf pan. Bake at 375 degrees for 50 minutes or until loaf tests done. Cool in pan for 10 minutes. Remove to wire rack to cool completely before slicing. **Yield:** 12 servings.

Strawberry-Nut Bread

4 eggs
1 cup oil
2 cups sugar
2   10-ounce packages frozen sliced
    strawberries, thawed
3 cups flour
1 tablespoon cinnamon
1 teaspoon baking soda
1 teaspoon salt
1 1/4 cups chopped pecans

Beat eggs in medium bowl until fluffy. Stir in oil, sugar and strawberries. Sift flour, cinnamon, baking soda and salt into large bowl. Mix in strawberry mixture. Fold in pecans. Pour into 2 greased and floured 5x9-inch loaf pans. Bake at 350 degrees for 1 hour and 10 minutes or until loaves test done. Cool in pans for 10 minutes. Remove to wire rack to cool completely. Chill before slicing. **Yield:** 24 servings.

FUN!
FUN!
FUN!

"Portable feasts and packable fun!"

✻ Don't cook up anything but fun. Visit your favorite deli and create an instant picnic.

✻ Have a picnic anywhere—the park, the porch, the backyard. Raining? Try the den.

✻ Spread an unusual tablecloth such as a quilt, cotton rug or open sleeping bag. Use bandannas for napkins.

✻ Fix a picnic in a sand pail for little ones. Tie a helium balloon to the handle for fun.

✻ Pack a picnic in your backpack; tuck in a new novel. Hike or bike to the perfect secluded spot and indulge yourself.

✻ Take along computer games or personal tape players with headphones to entertain children quietly in the car.

✻ Bake cakes or cookies in a 9x13-inch baking pan with sliding lid. Use the covered pan as a lap desk or game board in the car. Use the lid as a tray at the picnic.

Index

ACCOMPANIMENTS
Barbecued Apples, 79
Cajun Spice Mix, 75
Cool-in-the Kitchen Salsa, 66
Easy Pepper Medley, 65
Grilled Herb Potatoes, 78
Grilled Pear and Banana Kabobs, 79
Grilled Stuffed Mushrooms, 77
Grilled Zucchini, 78
Jezebel Sauce, 60
Quick Apple-Pepper Relish, 66
Speedy Squashickles, 67
Spicy Mayonnaise, 72
Tangy Uncooked Relish, 60
Tomato Topping, 72
Vegetable Care Packages, 78
APPETIZERS
Creamy Bacon Bars, 84
Dips, 83
Sausage Balls, 83
Vegetable Bars, 83
BEEF
Cow Patties, 84
Grilled Flank Steak, 71
Outdoor Tenderloin, 73
Spicy Steak, 72
Summertime Beef Kabobs, 71
BEVERAGES
Aloha Punch, 22
Apple Punch, 22
Banana-Chocolate Shake, 27
Blueberry Mountain, 20
Choco-Mint Shake, 27
Coffee Punch, 22
Cranberry-Cantaloupe Shake, 27
Cranberry-Pineapple Punch, 23
Cranberry Punch, 23
Cranberry Sparkle Punch, 23
Easy Party Punch, 24
Four-Fruit Party Punch, 24
Garden Club Punch, 25
Hawaiian Lemonade, 21
Kiwi-Yogurt Smoothie, 20
Mint Jewett, 21
Orange Julius, 21
Perky Pink Punch, 25
Pineapple-Citrus Punch, 25
Red Ice Cream Punch, 25
Slush, 29
Slushy Fruit Punch, 26
Sparkling Limeade, 21
Spiced Orange Frost, 28
Strawberry Swirl, 28
Strawberry-Yogurt Shake, 28
Summer Fruit Punch, 26
Tea, 29, 70
Yellow Daffodil Punch, 24
BREADS
Coconut-Orange Bread, 92
Parsley-Cheese French Bread, 79
Strawberry-Nut Bread, 92
CANDIES
Captain Crunch Candy, 43
Chocolate-Oatmeal Candy, 43
Coconut-Peanut Butter Balls, 46
Fudge, 44, 45

Graham Toffee Squares, 45
Hopscotch Crunchies, 45
Mashed Potato Candy, 47
Microwave Pralines, 47
Peanut Butter, 46, 47
Rocky Road Candy, 48

COOKIES
Almond Bars, 33
Brownies, 33, 34
Butterscotch Icebox Cookies, 36
Chocolate Caramel Layer Squares, 36
Chocolate Chip, 37
Chocolate Dump Bars, 37
Chocolate-Peanut Butter Bars, 38
Easiest Lemon Cookies, 39
Easy Peanut Butter Cookies, 40
Gooey Butter Cake Bars, 39
Lace Cookies, 38
Lemon Squares, 40
Marshmallow Brownies, 35
Oh Henry Bars, 40
Pecan Brownies, 34
Perfect Sugar Cookies, 42
Potato Chip Cookies, 41
Presto Snack Bars, 41
Prize-Winning Butter Brickle Bars, 35
S'mores, 32
Soda Cracker Caramel Bars, 42
Sour Cream Cookies, 41
Swedish Jam Bars, 43

FROZEN DESSERTS
Brownie Ice Cream Sandwiches, 18
Buster Bar Dessert, 11
Butter Brickle Dessert, 12
Butterfinger Delight, 12
Butterscotch Dessert, 13
Candy Bar Pie, 13
Chocolate Ice Cream Dessert, 14
Chocolate Malt Ice Cream Torte, 15
Chocolate-Cherry Ice Cream Dessert, 14
Chocolate-Coated Ice Cream Sandwiches, 19
Cool and Easy Ice Cream Dessert, 15
Crispy Ice Cream Dessert, 16
Dragon Dream Pops, 17
Frozen Fudge Sundae Dessert, 6
Frozen Strawberry Squares, 20
Mint Ice Cream Pies, 16
Neopolitan Ice Cream Sandwich Cake, 6
No-Drip Popsicles, 18
Oreo-Cherry Delight, 16
Peanut Buster Parfait, 17
Peppermint Ice Cream Pie, 17
Strawberry Delight, 19

ICE CREAM
Butter Pecan Ice Cream, 7, 8
Cherry Mash Ice Cream, 9
Coffee Ice Cream, 7
Date-Pecan Ice Cream Topping, 11
Easy Homemade Chocolate Ice Cream, 7
Lemon Ice Cream, 9
Mint Chocolate Chip Ice Cream, 7
Peppermint Candy Ice Cream, 7
Strawberry Ice Cream, 7, 10
Strawberry Sorbet, 9
The Best Ice Cream, 8
Vanilla Ice Cream, 7, 10, 11

JAMS AND JELLIES
Cherry-Zucchini Jam, 62
Fresh Kiwifruit Jam, 62
Grape Freezer Jelly, 63
Microwave Pepper and Honey Jelly, 64

Peachy Berry Jam, 64
Pepper Jelly to the Third Power, 65
Processor Apricot-Pineapple Jam, 61
Slow Cooker Apple Butter, 61
Strawberry and Raspberry Jam, 63
Ten-Minute Spiced Blueberry Jam, 62
Zucchini Marmalade, 63

PORK
Oriental Pork Chops, 73
Wonderful Ribs, 73

POULTRY
Barbecued Chicken, 74
Great Grilled Chicken, 74
Grilled Turkey Tenderloin, 75
Pepper Jelly Chicken, 74
Ribbon Sandwiches, 87
Spanish Pepper Chicken, 70

SALADS
Antipasto Salad, 88
Cauliflower Salad, 89
Copper Carrots, 88
Four-Bean Salad, 89
Marinated Green Beans, 90
Pasta Vinaigrette Salad, 90
Peach Salad, 91
Slaw, 67, 89
Sunny Fruit Salad, 91
Veggie Salad, 91

SANDWICHES
Chicken Croissants, 85
Cucumber Sandwiches, 85
Cyclers Sub, 82
Devilish Mini-Sandwiches, 85
Dried Beef Sandwich Filling, 86
Ham Delights, 86
Pecan-Cream Cheese Sandwiches, 86
Picnic Sandwiches, 87
Ribbon Sandwiches, 87
Sour Cream-Ham Sandwiches, 88
Tuna Salad Filling, 87

SEAFOOD
Bacon-Stuffed Trout, 76
Banana-Dijon Grilled Shrimp, 77
Italian Grilled Orange Roughy, 76
Marinated Fish Filets, 75
Marinated Shrimp, 84
Stuffed Flounder, 76

SNACKS
Can't-Just-Eat-One Crackers, 51
Chunky Puppy Chow, 48
Danish Pecans, 56
Dilly Smackers, 52
Easy Cheese Straws, 51
Granola, 52
Harvest Popcorn, 57
Mexican Munch, 52
Mini Ritz Cracker Snack, 51
My Favorite Trash, 49
Nibble Mix, 53
Niblets, 53
Onion Pretzels, 57
Party Mix, 54, 55
Poppy Chow, 48
Spiced Mixed Nuts, 53
Spiced Pecans, 56
Spiced Pretzels, 57
Sugar-Glazed Walnuts, 56
Sweet and Spicy Almonds, 50
Sweet Crispix Mix, 49
White Chocolate Crunch, 50
Yummy Bars, 50